THE CORPORATE COMMUNICATOR'S QUICK REFERENCE

THE CORPORATE COMMUNICATOR'S QUICK REFERENCE

PETER LICHTGARN

BUSINESS ONE IRWIN
Homewood, Illinois 60430

This publication is designed to provide accurate and
authoritative information in regard to the subject matter
covered. It is sold with the understanding that neither the
author nor the publisher is engaged in rendering legal, accounting,
or other professional service. If legal advice or other expert
assistance is required, the services of a competent
professional person should be sought.

*From a Declaration of Principles jointly adopted by a Committee
of the American Bar Association and a Committee of Publishers.*

Sponsoring editor: Cynthia A. Zigmund
Project editor: Carol L. Rose
Production manager: Ann Cassady
Jacket designer: Image House, Inc.
Compositor: BookMakers
Typeface: 11/14 Palatino
Printer: Book Press, Inc.

Library of Congress Cataloging-in-Publication Data

Lichtgarn, Peter.
  The corporate communicator's quick reference / Peter Lichtgarn.
    p.   cm.
  Includes index.
  ISBN 1-55623-892-4
  1. Communication in management. I. Title.
HD30.3.L5 1993
658.4'5—dc20   92–42083

Printed in the United States of America
1 2 3 4 5 6 7 8 9 0 BP 0 9 8 7 6 5 4 3

Preface

*T*he *Corporate Communicator's Quick Reference* is designed to help institute or refine a corporate communications program. This guide describes the duties, responsibilities, and functions necessary to act as liaison among service providers, the press, and employee and external audiences on the one hand and management or clients on the other. *The Corporate Communicator's Quick Reference* details the kinds of questions to ask and the type of performance to expect of employers, clients, vendors, and reporters while managing this vital function.

The first chapter, "Understanding Corporate Communications," establishes and defines the basic principles that every communicator must comprehend. It also underscores the operative tensions and dynamics inherent in the role.

Chapter two addresses an amorphous but equally vital topic, the concept of corporate culture. This chapter reveals how to grasp and make use of the subtleties of a given work environment.

The next seven chapters offer practical facts and guidelines for the specialized fields that a communicator encounters daily. Included are check lists, real-world advice, and sample forms that concern everything from graphic design to media relations, from events planning to videography.

Chapter ten discusses corporate communications as a career. It offers useful insights for those about to embark upon this specialty as well as for those fortunate enough to be practicing currently in this essential and ever-changing profession.

The chronology of corporate communications presented in the final chapter provides valuable background for the active or prospective practitioner. Knowing and understanding the historical context of your chosen area of interest adds value to your professional status.

Peter Lichtgarn

Acknowledgments

I had the pleasure and good fortune to consult several business communications experts while preparing this book. I sincerely appreciate the cooperation and encouragement I received from Jeff Goldschen, Lon Harding, DeAnn Kato, Laura Morgan, Lisa Cleri Reale, Craig St. Clair, and David Wogahn.

Eve Lichtgarn deserves a special note of thanks for her unerring judgment and good advice.

P.L.

Contents

One

Understanding Corporate Communications

C orporate communications are often confused with public relations. While it is true that corporate communications responsibilities often parallel those of a public relations
department, the difference between the two is pronounced.
Public relations functions usually concentrate on the individual client or the client's product or service. Corporate communications emphasize the message.

Corporate communications are informational media (print,
video, audio, or virtually any other medium) produced as an
integral part of daily business operations. This branch of communications is designed for internal use, external use, or both.
Directed to a defined, specifically targeted, or special audience

(e.g., shareholders, employees, managers, senior management, financial analysts, or any combination of these), corporate communications are often required or mandated by regulatory agencies. The Securities and Exchange Commission clearly describes when annual reports, quarterly reports, 10Ks and other financial information must be distributed and the specific information that those documents must contain.

Corporate communications sell corporate image and culture. Individual pieces of corporate communication directly reflect, enhance, and reinforce those corporate cultural traits. The pervasive influence of corporate communications begins with annual reports, affects common professional essentials such as business cards (often the first piece of corporate communication one encounters), and reaches such extremes as the color of cocktail napkins and the decision between cloth restroom towels embroidered with the company logo or stamped paper towels.

DUAL AWARENESS

Corporate communications require a balance of art and technology. You have to be aware of the means to most effectively and economically present your message and how to distribute it. Which media or method would best present your information: bulletin, flier, brochure, magazine, live announcement, video? Should the message be placed on desks, tacked to bulletin boards, or presented at employee meetings?

The most pronounced duality of a corporate communications career is the balance that must be maintained between business responsibilities and creativity. The business side is expensive. Creating art is expansive. One is easily codified, the other is intangible and indefinable. One is linear and allows no deviation from an established pattern, the other requires experience, understanding and the ability to think in the abstract. Yet, both are vital elements in corporate communications decision making.

The business side requires that attention be given to the following factors:

- Cost considerations.
- Choices for presentation (which media to use for maximum communication value and impact).
- Negotiating contracts, rights, permissions, use agreements, licenses, fee payments.
- The decision to hire (and pay) professional models or actors or to use employees in photos (or video).
- Determining those vendors best suited for your job. You may need to hire a photographer who specializes in portraits rather than product photography, or in architecture, food, panoramic scenery, or some other subject matter.

The creative side, on the other hand, is both a boon and a bane. It is a boon because the creativity you already demonstrated has impressed your boss or client sufficiently to get you a job or assignment. A communicator sells creativity. Talent distinguishes you from your many competitors.

Your creative side leads you to produce unique messages, but beware. Creativity is also the aspect of your personality that may very quickly increase production costs. Should you shoot photos on location or opt for studio photo sessions? Should you shoot in your city, or do you need to travel? Would film present a better feel than video?

Equally important is the fact that your creative side (which develops each time you exercise it) helps you solve problems.

Problems cost money. Solutions save money, and saving money pleases clients and bosses. There is a solution for every communications problem. Your job is to find the solution.

THREE GOALS

There are three goals of corporate communications.

Effectiveness

Your information must be received and understood by the audience.

Persuasiveness

Your information will cause an audience to act or react. Examples of persuasiveness include an artfully worded press release designed to quell rumors circulating in the media; an employee bulletin urging participation in a newly enhanced or recently restructured health benefit plan; reprints of the chairperson's speech created to quell press speculation and prove that the chairperson is firmly in charge of the business.

Adherence to Budget

Your boss (in an organizational setting) or your client (if you provide corporate communications services independently) will always ask about the cash value. The most frequently asked question is, "What is it going to cost?" Consider the cost to your company or client as part of an effective communications plan.

MEETING THE GOALS

As communication technology becomes more pervasive and accessible, new information dissemination opportunities become available that meet the three goals outlined. For example, consider satellite teleconferencing. The use of satellites and fixed-venue meetings satisfies economic, artistic, and technological issues at the same time. Satellite teleconferencing is economical because people don't have to travel—only the messages move. This is technologically appealing because the medium's interactive capabilities allow everyone to participate simultaneously. There is artistic satisfaction in controlling the images being transmitted.

One venerable accounting firm successfully utilized teleconferencing technology when it planned a three-day companywide employee meeting. This Los Angeles-based company maintained offices in nine cities around the country, although more than half of its 1,400 employees worked in the Southern California headquarters. The two main goals on the meeting's agenda were to introduce important new company procedures and to create a friendly atmosphere to combat a rising sense of isolation from the field offices.

At first, all field office employees at the level of manager and above were to be invited to the gathering. Two problems became apparent immediately. First, the cost of logistics proved too great. Budget projections for airfares, hotel expenses, and food bills were deemed too high even before the company factored in the costs of ground transportation and at least one evening's entertainment for the group. Second, almost a quarter of the company's employees would be excluded if only managers were invited.

In one planning session, the accounting firm's resourceful director of corporate communications proposed that the meeting be presented via teleconference. That meant that it could be presented live in Los Angeles and broadcast simultaneously to the company's field offices. The corporate communications department began to research this novel meeting concept. The communications staff defined the requirements: cameras, microphones, and television monitors at both the origination site and the receiving venues and the ability to send the electronic signals.

Eventually, the accounting firm engaged a turnkey tele- conferencing company, which provided necessary equip- ment at each office, rented time on a broadcast satellite to transmit the broadcast, and arranged for delivery of the electronic signal to designated locations. The service also included camera operators, sound technicians, and pro- duction specialists who performed the same service as the director of a televised news program. One added benefit was the ability to employ such supplemental visuals as video clips, slides, and illustrations during the presenta- tions.

Presenting the meeting as a teleconference solved sev- eral problems for the accounting firm. Management was impressed by the event's relative economy; the cost of hiring a teleconferencing vendor was considerably less than the amount originally projected for travel expenses. Be- cause the meeting came to the employees (both in Los Angeles and in field offices) instead of the traditional reverse, the interruption to productivity was slight. Most importantly, the teleconference proved to be a medium that allowed everyone (management and support staff) to receive information concurrently and to participate equally.

RESPONSIBILITIES

The responsibilities of a corporate communications depart- ment may involve several business disciplines.

Internal Communications

Such communications are directed to employees and operating unit management. They include bulletins, announcements, company or client magazine, pamphlets, brochures, or fliers.

External Communications and Media Relations

Publications, stationery, programs, and press releases created for audiences outside the organization constitute external communications. The liaison function between your company or client and the news and information organizations constitutes media relations. The individual responsible for these communication tasks becomes your company's or client's spokesperson. To assign these responsibilities to someone with clout, such as a corporate officer, enhances the credibility of the communications.

Investor Relations

This is a specialized area that serves the financial and investment communities exclusively.

Government Relations

In legislative centers on the federal, state, or local levels, the government relations staff monitors legislation, lobbies for or against pending legislation, and provides your company's or client's response to regulatory issues.

Special Projects and Event Planning

This function assumes responsibility for a full range of social events including luncheons, dinners, assemblies, diplomatic receptions, press tours, employee service awards, and holiday parties.

The number of corporate communications staff members in a department depends, of course, on the size of the organization. In large, stratified companies, which can afford to maintain big staffs, individual corporate communicators may be specialized. That is, one person may perform a single communications function, writing only press releases, or working entirely in the video department, or writing exclusively for the company magazine.

Some companies, however, prefer the multifunctional staff. Communicators in this environment contribute a portion of their expertise to a range of communications functions. An individual could participate in the concept, copy writing, and art direction of a publication, as well as in media relations and special events planning.

The corporate communicator strives to deliver useful information via media that are interesting to read, see, or hear. Audience acceptance of a message directly correlates with the quality of the medium by which the message is delivered—the package must beckon. However, it is important to guard against inappropriateness. For instance, a company should not engrave pink slips or publish a four-color glossy employee magazine during a period of layoffs.

PRODUCTS AND SERVICES

A corporate communications department may be asked to create an ambitious array of products, including (but not limited to) the following categories.

Print Materials

These include annual reports, quarterly reports, magazines, speech reprints, trade ads, rosters, programs, posters, and invitations.

Photography, Art, or Graphics

This is one area where the need to understand both business and art is most acute. Many photographers, artists, and graphic designers deal in abstracts. The practical considerations of business are remote to many creative personalities. It is the job of the corporate communicator to link business with art, to be conversant with the ways of both worlds.

Video

Creating video can be an entire career unto itself. However, you can successfully produce corporate video with technical assistance and some essential background information:

- Audiences are familiar with video.
- More people will watch corporate information than will read it.
- Video is cost-effective, depending on the size of your audience and the expected use of the video.
- Video production costs are often competitive with print costs.

Multi-Image Shows

Slide shows combined with live performance add dynamism and excitement to annual meetings, sales conferences, employee morale shows, or product introductions. Multi-image is best for big audiences because the images are very large, very bold, and very expensive. However, multi-image shows are also hard to control and synchronize. If one of the projectors in a 12-projector show is jiggled out of alignment, the soundtrack is one slide off, or the slide tray gets stuck, the entire presentation is an irretrievable mess.

Technology-Dependent Communications

These are exotic communications media that include teleconferences, satellite deliveries, electronic mail systems, CD-ROMs, data bases, and computer graphics. You may need help creating such media. To find assistance ask colleagues, check with your advertising agency contacts for leads, or refer to specialized media directories.

INFORMATION SOURCES

Project ideas come from many sources:

- Your own original ideas.
- The idea of your employer, client, peers, colleagues, or business acquaintances.
- Your observations and conversations as you travel through your office, building, factory, store, business meeting, etc.
- Business and consumer media—mainly broadcasts, newspapers, magazines, and professional publications.
- Trade associations or professional society meetings.
- Public relations departments.
- Input or suggestions from outside the company.
- Surveys.
- Clipping services.

DISTRIBUTION MEDIA

There are many factors to consider in selecting distribution media:

- Which are available?
- Which are best suited for a particular project?
- Which would you like to use or create?
- Which would you avoid?
- Which will serve you and your client or boss best (considering finances, timeliness, credibility, and presentation)?

There are several distribution options to investigate. You may choose to utilize one or several existing options or institute your own self-designed program.

Publications/Print Media

These may target an entire employee population or only certain segments, such as managers, transportation crews, night-shift workers, region-specific operations staff, or retirees. Publications and print media may include brochures, bulletin board messages, posters, or flyers; reminders such as envelope stuffers, tabletop tent cards, or novelties (balloons, pens, T-shirts, etc.).

Electronic Media

An organization may produce and distribute audio and video programs. These may be formal programs, such as video magazines, or informal, unscheduled programs. Frequently, these presentations are designed to highlight new company policies. For instance, to emphasize a new companywide smoke-free environment, a corporate communicator may arrange for a video explaining the benefits of the new program to play in the employee cafeteria for a week. Other electronic media include:

- Complaint/suggestion telephone lines.
- Toll-free telephone numbers.
- Public-address system announcements.
- Electronic mail.

Live Information Exchanges

Information is distributed among individuals face-to-face in situations such as:

- Press relations programs.
- Companywide meetings.
- Advisory boards made up of employees or customers.
- Awards and employee recognition programs.

AUDIENCES

Your communications programs should be designed to reach a specific audience. Identify audiences by their unifying characteristics and concerns. Recognizing audiences' common interests allows you to plan messages accordingly. Be aware that areas of interest vary by audience. For instance, an executive-level audience may place great value on information regarding management techniques or company image while hourly wage earners may be more interested in success stories and in professional development possibilities than in excerpts of remarks by the senior vice president of employee relations.

Employee-Audience Concerns

The top three topics that will capture the interest of virtually every employee demographic are:

- Finances (personal before organizational). People want information about how they are doing versus how the company is performing.
- Industry comparisons. Employees also like to know how their compensation or productivity compares with their peers at competing companies.
- Their jobs. Employees want to feel they can progress in their jobs, be promoted, and expand their influence beyond its present bounds.

Other topics of interest to employee audiences include:

- Their organization. Is their industry shrinking or growing?
- Perceived or real problems and their remedies.
- Short- and long-term strategies.
- The senior executive staff and its method of decision making.

THE BEST PRODUCT

Every communications program shares basic traits. To attain success, they all must be researched, planned, produced, and distributed. Each of these categories benefits from—indeed requires—the corporate communicator's special blend of artistic and business knowledge.

During the research phase, feasibility becomes the core issue. Is it possible to begin this project? Is it necessary? If the answers are yes, the planning period begins. How will a message be presented? To whom? Is a deluxe package affordable or will greater economy be received favorably? The next step includes selection of communication service providers:

graphic designers, photographers, printers, and the like. Finally, but no less important, are the method and environment in which messages are delivered. The best advice for presenting effective communications is to keep them simple and short.

Research, planning, production, and distribution have direct impact on the materials produced. These four phases are not inherently complicated, but they must not be overlooked. The information gained from these processes helps ensure that the best product possible will be presented, given the company's or client's financial instructions, cultural nuances, and distribution parameters. On an emotional level, the creativity and attention to detail evident in any project shows respect for readers, viewers, respondents, or guests.

The business procedures applied to manage the creative process underscore the importance of the professional communicator. Serving as the link between abstract and empirical knowledge is only one of many ways communicators add value to the organization's goals.

Two

Corporate Culture

C orporate culture is a phrase that has been used previously in this book, but defining it is no simple task. In
order to get a grasp of the concept of corporate culture, it is
necessary to study a variety of factors that tend to be intangible in nature—factors such as image, attitude, demeanor,
values, and beliefs. From components such as these, a corporate culture can be gleaned, interpreted, and deduced by the
keen observer.

Determining corporate culture is not an exact science. Yet
it is essential for a professional communicator to be able to
define this concept in the context of his or her own corporate
environment. The difference between the ability and inabil-
ity to do so can be as basic as the difference between triumph
and disaster in times of crisis management. Some examples
will illustrate this point later in the chapter.

First, it may be helpful to see how the modern business
press defines corporate culture. It has been described as the
basic values, assumptions, goals, and beliefs that guide the

way the corporation operates.[1] Corporate culture has been referred to as the special mix of knowledge, experience, skills, expertise, and attitude that distinguishes the organization and determines its ability to create value in the marketplace.[2] It has also been characterized as "the values, heroes, myths, symbols that have been in the organization forever, the attitudes that say, 'Don't disagree with the boss,' or 'Don't make waves,' or 'Just do enough to get by,' or 'For God's sake, don't take chances.'"[3]

How do you go about determining the culture of a given corporate environment? Realistically, these factors are rarely, if ever, directly talked about by employees. Materials prepared by human resource departments often sidestep the topic altogether. The cultures of companies with high-profile products or services need special scrutiny. Do not confuse a heavy advertising presence or product association with that organization's work environment.

In order to bring underlying cultural factors to the surface, consider yourself a type of anthropologist. Observe the behavior and appearance of others as you explore the corporate environment. Pick up clues, and be aware of attitudes. Certain elements or situations will help reveal a company's culture.

Read, study, and analyze print and video pieces such as annual and quarterly reports, brochures, newsletters, press releases, employee orientation videos, speeches, advertising or product description materials.

---

[1]"Culturing Change," *The Economist*, July 7, 1990, p. 65.

[2]Patrick J. Smith, "How to Present Your Firm to the World," *The Journal of Business Strategy* (January/February 1990), p. 32.

[3]Brian Dumaine, "Creating a New Company Culture," *Fortune*, January 15, 1990, p. 127.

Observe the physical environment. In what condition do you find the offices and public areas? Is there a clean-desk policy? Is there a rule about what you can hang on the walls? Is food allowed in the work areas?

Listen to how the employees speak. Language reveals much about an organization. How do people answer the phones? Do people swear in the office?

Observe how people dress. Is the typical office attire "button-down" or casual?

Determine the relationship between employees and management. Are superiors addressed on a first-name basis? Is access to superiors limited, or is there an open-door policy? Are meetings arranged on a drop-in basis or by invitation only? Is attendance mandatory or optional? Is there an organizational chart?

Discover how the company treats its employees. Do entrepreneurial attitudes exist, or are employees just told what to do? Are there orientation programs, training seminars, reward systems, recognition dinners, bonuses, retirement ceremonies, or succession plans? Are company-sponsored social events "beer busts" or formal affairs?

Determine whether privileges or perquisites serve to unite or separate levels of employees. Are there reserved parking spaces? Is there an executive dining room or a common lunch room? Does the company have a gym? Who is eligible to use it? Do members of senior management participate in the company-sponsored employee social functions? Are executives visible? Does the organization buy season tickets to cultural or sporting events? Who is entitled to use them?

Each corporate culture, like each identifiable society, is unique. This is what makes a definition so elusive. Despite all the intangible ingredients that go into the making of a corporate culture, often one element is discernible and obtainable—usually in writing. It is called a mission statement.

MISSION STATEMENTS

In the mid-1980s, the trend to codify a corporation's purpose, beliefs, and aspirations became fashionable for organizations of all sizes. These written credos are known as mission statements.

The benefit of a mission statement is its undisputed declaration of the essence of the company and the tenets to which it adheres. It can serve as a unifying force for employees by providing a cohesiveness and fraternity that make a more pleasant work environment, enhance morale, and lead to increased productivity. The mission statement allows employees to see the "big picture," the larger scheme of company activities beyond their individual jobs. It can establish a platform for managers to feel good about what they do. A mission statement is an announcement that the corporation has a soul.

The weakness of a mission statement is its remoteness from everyday operations. It is impractical for a business communicator to consult the corporate mission statement for an immediate solution to a specific problem. There is a tendency to write these declarations in such stilted, lofty tones that employees find them useless, or, worse yet, a source of amusement.

Most mission statements mention employees, the organization's goals, its responsibility to shareholders, and, often, the duty a company feels toward the community in which it operates.

The following sections present some sample mission statements.

Johnson & Johnson

We believe that our first responsibility is to the doctors, nurses, hospitals, mothers, and all others who use our products. Our products must always be of the highest quality. We must constantly strive to reduce the cost of these products. Our orders must be promptly and accurately filled. Our dealers must make a fair profit.

Our second responsibility is to those who work with us—the men and women in our plants and offices. They must have a sense of security in their jobs. Wages must be fair and adequate, management just, hours reasonable, and working conditions clean and orderly. Employees should have an organized system for suggestions and complaints. Supervisors and department heads must be qualified and fair minded. There must be opportunity for advancement—for those qualified and each person must be considered an individual standing on his own dignity and merit.

Our third responsibility is to our management. Our executives must be persons of talent, education, experience and ability. They must be persons of common sense and full understanding.

Our fourth responsibility is to the communities in which we live. We must be a good citizen—support good works and charity, and bear our fair share of taxes. We must maintain in good order the property we are privileged to use. We must participate in promotion of civic improvement, health, education and good government, and acquaint the community with our activities.

Our fifth and last responsibility is to our stockholders. Business must make a sound profit. Reserves must be created, research must be carried on, adventurous programs developed, and mistakes paid for. Adverse times must be provided for, adequate taxes paid, new machines purchased, new plants built, new products launched, and new sales plans developed. We must experiment with new ideas. When these things have been done the stockholder should receive a fair return. We are determined with the help of God's grace, to fulfill these obligations to the best of our ability.

Notice how the corporate allegiances are structured in a clear hierarchy. Also notice that the obligation to pay adequate taxes is mentioned not once, but twice.

The Times Mirror Company

The Times Mirror Company is committed to gathering and disseminating the information people need to live, work and govern themselves in a free society.

We will strive to do so with the highest standards of accuracy, fairness, quality and timeliness.

In pursuing this mission, we will constantly strive to strike an appropriate balance among the following objectives:

Continue to grow in size and stature as to ensure a preeminent national scope, reach and voice.

Preserve corporate independence and stability provided by substantial Chandler family [the company's founders] and employee stock ownership.

Provide above-average total financial return— share-price appreciations plus dividends—for shareholders over the long term.

Maintain conservative risk posture, and hence, financial flexibility.

Enhance our position as a leading force among American newspaper groups.

Balance newspaper holdings with significant positions in related communications and information fields, including magazines, broadcast television, cable television, and professional information and book publishing.

Attract, motivate and retain a high-quality workforce that reflects the diversity of our society, and provide a positive work environment that allows employees' talents to be developed to the fullest.

Provide independent editorial voices. Contribute to the economic and social well-being of the communities we serve.

Notice the echoes of First Amendment sensibilities.

Budget Rent A Car

We are committed to providing legitimate value and exceptional service to our customers by renting, leasing, wholesaling, retailing, and transporting clean, safe vehicles while creating a profitable and continuously growing Company.

We are committed to offering rewarding employment opportunities and advancement through achievement in a supportive work environment. We recognize that motivated and dedicated employees are our Company's greatest resource.

We also are committed to fulfilling our declaration toward improving the quality of life for all people by our dedication to eliminating the persistence of hunger in the world.

Mission statements can be surprising; here is a car rental service dedicated to eradicating world hunger.

Mission statements require maintenance. As the business environment changes, as the corporation adapts, the mission statement can grow old, obsolete, or ineffective. Just because they sound as if they are carved in stone doesn't mean they are. They can, and should, be updated and made relevant. It is logical for the corporate communicator to assume this task. Utilize the mission statement as a vehicle for introduction to senior executives in order to discuss adaptation or change. Keep in mind that mission statements are useful hooks on which to hang future ideas and proposals.

CORPORATE CULTURE AND COMMUNICATIONS

Earlier in this chapter it was mentioned that the communicator's attention or inattention to the given corporate culture can spell the difference between victory and defeat when it comes to handling sensitive or catastrophic events. Vividly illustrating the interaction between corporate culture and communications are the distinctly different responses of two companies to well-publicized tragedies that threatened their image, profitability, and future operations.

The Exxon Valdez

In the spring of 1989, the oil tanker Exxon *Valdez* ran aground in Prince William Sound, Alaska, and spilled 11 million gallons of crude into the bay. For days following the accident, seemingly nothing was done to staunch the flow of oil or contain the slick.

The corporation itself was uncommunicative. There was no immediate press conference scheduled, and no statements were forthcoming from management. In fact, the CEO, Lawrence Rawl, was conspicuous in his absence. Although the public and the press had expected him to go to the spill site and show some concern, he did not. It wasn't until a week after the incident that Rawl stepped into public view. (One of the more damaging, and unfortunate, official quotations regarding the incident came from Rawl well after the accident occurred. He explained his failure to go to Alaska by saying the cleanup was in capable hands and that he had "many other things to do.")

Exxon communications suffered a cultural breakdown. The silence of the corporate voice only projected an attitude of indifference. This was especially disappointing from a company that had spent billions of dollars over the years to promote its product and enhance its image.

The public—both consumers and investors—disapproved mightily of Exxon's poor display of crisis management. People began cutting up their Exxon credit cards. Before the spill, Exxon rated 6th on *Fortune* magazine's list of America's most admired corporations. After the spill, it plummeted to 110th place.

In an interview given a couple of months after the *Valdez* accident, Rawl admitted that—on a surface level at least—he erred by not traveling to Prince William Sound right away. "From a public relations standpoint, it probably would have been better had I gone up there," he said.[4] However, Rawl remained defensive about Exxon's actions immediately after the spill, and he blamed the Coast Guard and "environmentalists" (the label Rawl used) for not allowing Exxon to drop chemical dispersants on the growing slick. Comments such as these underscored Exxon's refusal to acknowledge its own

---

[4] "In Ten Years You'll See 'Nothing,'" *Fortune*, May 8, 1989, p. 50.

employee's negligence in allowing the tanker to go aground, as well as its continuing reluctance to accept responsibility for the consequences.

When asked if he had advice for other corporations facing a crisis, Rawl said, "You'd better prethink which way you are going to jump from a public affairs standpoint before you have any kind of a problem. You ought to always have a public affairs plan ...." This could be interpreted as a disturbing admission that a corporation as structured as Exxon had no such plan.

Exxon's response stands in sharp contrast to Johnson & Johnson's crisis communications management.

Tylenol

In 1982, seven people in the Chicago area died suddenly and mysteriously. Investigation revealed that these people had all taken Tylenol pain reliever just prior to their deaths and that the Tylenol had been laced with cyanide in an act of criminal product tampering.

Tylenol, manufactured by Johnson & Johnson, was the most successful over-the-counter pain relief product in the country. Immediately upon learning of the reported deaths and their connection with Tylenol, Johnson & Johnson:

- Recalled Tylenol from the market.
- Halted advertising and production of Tylenol.
- Investigated the manufacturing process.
- Set up communications networks to handle the media, consumers, health professionals, and employees.
- Requested the assistance of the Food and Drug Administration.

- Offered a reward to capture the tampering perpetrator.
- Conducted consumer surveys.
- Initiated industrywide efforts to develop tamper-resistant packaging.

In addition, the CEO and senior executives made themselves available to print and broadcast media so that correct information could be presented to the public. During the concentrated media coverage that ensued, Johnson & Johnson management accepted full responsibility, even though nothing in the manufacturing, packaging, or distribution of Tylenol was proven—or even alleged—to be the source of the problem. Their product had been chosen by an outsider as the vehicle for murder.

The entire crisis communications strategy worked brilliantly. The public's perception of the company was positive enough to allow reintroduction of Tylenol (with new packaging) the following year. Even though many industry analysts advised against reintroducing the product, Johnson & Johnson executives felt their quick response and free flow of information worked to minimize risk. When Tylenol came back, it recaptured nearly its total market share.

Robert Wood Johnson, the son of the company's founder, made the following statement in his book, *Or Forfeit Freedom:*

> American institutions, both public and private, exist because the people want them, believe in them, or at least are willing to tolerate them. The day has passed when business was a private matter—if it ever really was. In a business society, every act of business has social consequences and may arouse public interest. Every time business hires, builds, sells or buys, it is

acting for the American people as well as for itself, and
it must be prepared to accept full responsibility for its
acts.

The Johnson & Johnson reaction to the Tylenol tampering
has been cited as an exemplary display of how the communications department of a major corporation should perform
to control crises. Johnson & Johnson management has repeat-
edly said that, given their forthright corporate cultural heri-
tage, they could not have acted in any other way.

Three
Graphic Design

A graphic designer is, essentially, a translator who transforms your message into an audience-pleasing presentation. Designers help assemble the aesthetics, the look, the format, and the physical appearance of your print piece.

Graphic designers provide a wide variety of services. Some offer market input. Designers with this capability are usually armed with research showing why certain graphic choices are better than others, why photographs might look better than drawings, what colors might elicit better responses from your audience, which type sizes and styles to consider, and where to place headlines. While some designers are concerned only with aesthetic considerations, others work in teams to provide ancillary services. Some graphic design services function as mini-advertising agencies by providing copy editing, in-house photography, typesetting, and ad placement.

When selecting a designer, always inspect his or her portfolio, book, or slide show. Based on samples and rate structure, determine who will be best for a particular job. Designer A may be suited for production work; Designer B may produce work quickly but may not be as creative as Designer C, who is your choice for more complicated jobs.

After reviewing samples, ask the designer why and how a certain piece was assembled. Inquire about the results, marketing returns, or response rates. A knowledgeable graphic designer will know how a specific piece performed, but one of lesser experience won't know or care whether it performed well.

Before you interview one or two designers, you must assemble your thoughts about the project. First, define the demographics. Who is the target audience? Does it consist of consumers, customers, or professional peers? What are the predominant gender and age? Second, establish the purpose. Are you trying to impress customers or clients with capabilities? Do you want your audience to make a telephone call or mail in a coupon? Third, envision what kind of format you want. What would be the best size and dimensions? Should it fit into a number 10 envelope, or should it be a flat sheet suitable for mailing? Should the sheets be loose, folded, or saddle-stitched? What about the weight of the paper? How will your decisions affect postage costs? If you're not sure, leave your options open. The designer can help you come to the best solution.

BUDGET

How much can you spend? A budget will help the designer determine if the job you plan is too complicated for the money allotted. Most designers base their cost estimates on hours. Ask about these time considerations to estimate graphic design costs:

- How many hours will it take to assemble the project?
- How many panels or pages will it comprise?
- Will it include color or black and white photographs?
- Who will supply the photos or illustrations?
- Will the designer have to arrange for photo services or hire an illustrator?
- Do you want the designer to research photos and artwork for you?
- Do you want color comprehensives (comps)?
- What is the timeframe?

Specialized directories provide guidelines for graphic design costs. Print sources and word-of-mouth information from colleagues should give you a good idea whether you are paying fees above or below industry norms. There is a degree of subjectivity involved, however. Designers know how much time a given project will require, so their estimates often are based on experience with similar jobs.

Always get a firm estimate at the beginning of every job. The price you agree to pay for your job usually allows for one or two revisions of a given size. Beyond that, you may begin paying extra fees.

DESIGNER'S RESPONSIBILITY

The designer's responsibilities include:

- Providing a useful product created to suit your needs.

- Alerting you to cost escalation beyond the terms of your agreement.
- Describing what you should expect if you must exceed the limits of your agreement.

At the end of a project, your bill shouldn't exceed the amount agreed upon by more than a few percentage points. Most designers finish the job very close to the estimate.

The responsibilities of the designer as well as the client are listed in the chronology of a design project that appears at the end of this chapter.

TIME

After establishing a budget, create a time line. The creative process of graphic design takes time, and every designer works at a different speed. Allow one or two weeks for a good comp. Your job will probably be produced simultaneously with other clients' work. If yours is a rush job, make that clear. A rush job assumes higher priority, and a designer may or may not charge extra for the service. The designer's largesse usually depends on your relationship. A design house may waive rush charges for an established client.

QUANTITY

You should also decide the quantity in which your piece is to be printed. A small print run (up to 1,000 copies) will affect your graphic design plans. Four-color printing requires a substantial print run (at least 2,000) to be cost-effective. Cost amortization is pronounced at quantities of 10,000 to 15,000. Your designer can advise you about the relative size of the print run versus the cost of one-, two-, or four-color artwork.

Some graphic designers like to see what print pieces your company or client has produced in the past. You can explain why you liked or disliked a print piece or whether it was effective and well-received. This also gives the designer a chance to see the style your corporate culture encourages.

COMPREHENSIVES (COMPS)

Comprehensive artwork is presented to the client to show how the job will ultimately look. Comps can be either "loose" or "tight." A loose comp may consist of only a pencil sketch, if you (and everyone who needs to approve the project) can envision the final product from it. A tight comp, on the other hand, shows exactly how and where all the graphic elements will fit and what colors will be used.

Most clients want tight comps, comprising exact detail and precise presentation. The exactness of tight comps is essential for people who cannot visualize art concepts easily. Conversely, loose comps leave holes in the presentation and, possibly, in the concept. Loose comps are cheaper and faster but don't guarantee the position of pictures, headlines, or type. The prevalence of desktop design systems allows graphic designers to present eye-catching, tight comps for a fraction of the time and money required for cut-and-paste or pencil-rendered artboards.

BIDS AND ESTIMATES

Designers need information and details about your project to make an accurate bid. The more information you can provide the designer up front, the better. Useful information includes dimensions, intended use, the amount of materials you can provide, and your budget. The designer will synthesize the information and give you a job estimate, a timeline, and a schedule of production. (A sample cost estimate sheet appears at the end of this chapter.)

Telling your designer how many copies you anticipate printing is also important. The designer may create art assuming you will produce 25,000 copies. If you only need 500, your printing experience will be unnecessarily complicated and expensive. The more accurate and comprehensive your input, the better the designer's execution.

A bid is rarely changed by either party after it has been delivered. Your designer doesn't want to change the terms of the agreement because it is an uncomfortable situation, and most clients realize that it is difficult, bothersome, and complicated to resubmit the vendor paperwork their organizations require. Usually, everybody bends to make accommodation. There will often be certain things you have to include in your project post facto because a superior in your organization insists. In those cases, you may pay an extra hourly charge. Remember that copy and art changes become more expensive as the production cycle nears completion.

Have your copy approved (by senior management, legal counsel, department heads, other departments, or by anyone else who must be consulted) when you approach a designer for an estimate. He or she will base costs and assess presentation possibilities on the amount of copy submitted by the client. If the final version of the copy is longer than originally planned, the estimate is wrong and any preplanning is rendered useless.

Clients often think it wise to take the lowest bid from among three designers, but beware. You aren't always evaluating apples against apples. The experience of each design house differs, as do the level and scope of creativity. It may be beneficial to choose a designer first, discuss the amount you can spend, and work out an agreement. If the designer can't work within that price range, move to another designer.

TERMS

Billing

Graphic designers frequently bill new clients in three equal installments of one third each. Customarily, the client will pay the first third of a specific project's design costs when the job begins. The middle third is paid at some prearranged midpoint such as when comps are approved. The final third is paid when the completed job is delivered. Variations are common: payment may be made in full, in two installments of one half each, or in four installments of one fourth each. Terms are negotiable between the designer and the client.

Rights and Ownership

Do you, the designer, or the artist own the artwork? What rights does ownership entail? Who stores the artboards? These points vary and are negotiable for each job. Ask these questions to avoid future complications should you decide to reprint or reuse artwork, photos, or illustrations.

Kill Fees

Establish the guidelines both you and the designer will follow if a project is cancelled. Generally, if the design work has been completed or is close to completion, you can expect to pay the entire design fee. Whether you print the job is not the question. This protects the designer whose client has said, "Oh, we decided not to go forward with that piece. We'll call you when we're ready." If your project needs refreshing after a period of time, expect to pay another fee for additional service. The sum may be smaller than the first fee if a portion of the original work is salvageable.

This exact circumstance occurred to a graphic designer who was working with a new client. The designer had won a bid to produce a four-color, six-page brochure that described the client's holdings and areas of business. After a preliminary consultation session between the designer and the client's communications person, but before any work began, both parties signed a production agreement. Among such terms as due dates and billing procedures, the agreement included a provision for payment if the client decided to discontinue work on the brochure. This language in an agreement between a service provider and the client is commonly called the "kill fee" clause. That means the client agrees to pay the provider if the client kills, or terminates, the project.

Work began on the project and progressed as far as a second set of corrections. Circumstances dictated that essential financial figures would not be available for at least five months, so the client set aside the project for that period of time. However, he was unsure whether the brochure would be produced at all. Before contacting the designer, the client reviewed the production agreement both had signed and reexamined the kill fee section. When he reported the status of the brochure to the designer, he was prepared to pay her fee to date. Of course, the designer was disappointed that the project had been postponed but relieved that the client adhered to the terms of their agreement.

Six months later, the client revived the brochure project and called the designer to reengage her services. This new incarnation of the brochure required the designer to replace obsolete financial information—an easy task since her previously completed work was still usable. The client and designer mutually decided on an hourly fee arrangement to finish the brochure.

Experienced communicators plan for contingencies that may impede completion of a project. After the brochure was finished, both the graphic designer and the client agreed that the kill fee clause helped avoid embarrassment, confusion, and ill will.

WORKING WITH THE TOP

Virtually all service providers, including designers, would prefer to work with the ultimate decision maker, but they rarely do. You, as the communications expert, are generally the liaison between graphic suppliers and management. The reasons are practical: your superiors usually don't have the time or expertise to deal with the creative process. Often the ultimate decision maker isn't skilled in communications, photography, artwork, or graphic design. Worse, he or she could submit your project to a committee for approval.

A good practice, if possible, is to have the vendors meet the decision makers. Also, arrange to have the designer available during a corporate or client presentation. The designer has much more information about why and how the job was assembled the way it was. Virtually every service provider is willing to make a presentation to the highest officer available.

CORPORATE GRAPHIC IDENTITY

Graphic identity is the union of a company's or client's name, product, or service with a distinctive logo, trademark, service mark, color scheme, typeface, or style. Successful corporate emblems evoke an immediate thought association with a standard of service, quality, or value. To test this yourself, review the following list of companies and see if you can describe, draw, or visualize their logos, trademarks, or service symbols:

Apple Computers
United Airlines
Pepsi
MGM
Volkswagen
Your local telephone company

Each name suggests a familiar graphic representation.

A corporate logo and its use must not be taken lightly. The development and design of a logo undoubtedly represent a large investment. Its use in the marketplace is directly linked to consumer goodwill and investor confidence. Logos certainly require a great deal of money to maintain, and they could cost exponentially more to protect through litigation if challenged by infringement.

As a professional business communicator, you may participate in the creation of a graphic identity program. You will also become the source of proper logo-use information for your company or client. Consequently, it is up to you to use the mark correctly and within the parameters of your corporate graphic standards. If you use the logo incorrectly, you'll certainly hear about it from your legal department, from company veterans, (some pretty high up) who feel a kinship bond with it, or possibly from customers. Incorrect use weakens or, in extreme cases, invalidates your trademark or servicemark protection.

To help employees, graphic designers, outside vendors, or subsidiary graphic personnel use logos or trademarks correctly and uniformly, companies set out their rules in graphic standards manuals. These books contain rules for logo use in print, video, signage, on uniforms, packaging, vehicles, and in all other foreseeable manifestations.

Establish and maintain a single image for your company to which every department adheres. Uniform graphic images send the tacit message of a strong and cohesive organization.

Chronology of a Graphic Design Project

(1)   Client decides to begin project.

(2)   Client inspects prospective designers' portfolios.

(3)   Client chooses designer.

(4)   Client and designer agree to terms.

(5)   Client and designer share input.

(6)   Client pays one third of project design fee.

(7)   Designer produces comps.

(8)   Client inspects comps.

(9)   Client makes suggestions for revisions.

(10)   Designer finalizes graphic style.

(11)   Client makes second of three payments.

(12)   Designer orders type, photos or illustrations.

(13)   Designer pastes up artboards or prepares disk with computer-generated art.

(14)   Client proofreads artboards or reviews disk.

(15)   Designer makes corrections and revisions.

(16)   Client inspects corrections and revisions.

(17) Client approves artboards or material on disk.

(18) Client pays remaining balance of design fee.

(19) Designer delivers artboards or computer disk to printer.

Graphic design cost estimate sheet

Date _____

Client _____

Project title_____

Project description/design services required _____

_____

_____

_____

_____

Itemized expenses

Design time _____hours @ $_____ per hour $_____

Production time _____hours @ $_____ per hour $_____

Illustration/photography fees $_____

Material and supplies $_____

Photographic prints $_____

Printing $_____

Typesetting $_____

Photostats $_____

Messengers $_____

Shipping $_____

Other (specify) $_____

  TOTAL $_____

  Sales tax $_____

  GRAND TOTAL $_____

Four
Printing

J ust as you take mental notes about graphic designers, you should do the same with printers. There are several facts you will need to know.

First, you should determine how many colors can be printed in one pass on the printer's press. Is your printer a one-color, two-color, or four-color shop? Quick printers or small shops specializing in business cards and stationery usually utilize only one color at a time because their presses have only one roller. That means the paper has to be sent through the press separately for each color—twice through for two-color work, four times through for four-color jobs. Larger printers will have two-color or four-color presses, which can lay down two or four colors at once, respectively. Four-color printing is best done on a four-color press to avoid registration problems. There are some five-color presses, but presses with four-color or six-color capability are more common.

You should also consider how many of each press your printer has and what sizes those presses are. The size of the press determines the size of the paper. Consequently, if you have a long sheet, a quick printer may not accommodate it.

Printers specialize. A different printer will probably be required for different-sized jobs. In-house capabilities, press capacity, and technological skill vary. The printer who produces your stationery may not be able to handle a large printing job requiring hair-splitting precision.

BEFORE CHOOSING A PRINTER

Evaluate the printer by:

- Capabilities.
- Capacity.
- The number of colors that can be printed at one time.
- Whether the printer does specialty work (such as separations or binding) in-house.
- Experience as well as cost. Experienced printers usually have production tips they can share to help your job proceed smoothly.

OBTAINING A PRINTER'S BID

Before a printer can present a bid, you will need to provide the following information:

- A brief description of the job to be printed.
- The finished size.
- The number of pages.
- Which paper stock you want to buy.

- The number of copies to be printed.
- What kind and how many colors of ink you require.
- Whether there are any bleeds.
- Whether there are any screens.
- The number of halftones.
- The number of duotones.
- The number of color separations.
- Whether folding or scoring is required.
- The kind of binding (e.g., saddle stitching, perfect binding) you want.
- Whether you desire embossing, die cuts, foil, or other special applications.
- Packing instructions.
- Delivery/shipping instructions.
- Whether you will accept overs and unders.

One of the most important things you need to know about obtaining a bid is whether you are willing to pay the overs and unders charges. There is a convention that says a printer can deliver (and therefore charge you for) 10 percent more than (over) or 10 percent less than (under) the number of pieces you order. For example, if you agree to pay $2,000 for exactly 2,000 copies of your job, the printer may, under the terms of the agreement you probably signed, charge you $2,200 and give you 2,200 copies (200, or 10 percent more than the number requested) or charge you $1,800 and give you 1,800 copies (200, or 10 percent fewer than the number requested). Receiving fewer than expected could cause problems if you need exactly 2,000 copies.

The reasons for the under or over proviso involve issues of quality control (e.g., ink not laying down properly, registration problems) or stopping the press at an exact time (the press may print another 100 copies before it can be stopped).

This over and under clause is, of course, negotiable. If you are working on a strict budget and wish to pay only for an exact amount, specify your terms before the printing begins. Obtain a firm price and state that you will accept no overs, no unders. Expect to pay extra to exercise that option, because a printer will have to produce overs to satisfy your exact amount. Paying for fewer copies is rare. The advantage of specifying no overs, no unders is that the price will not change.

Most printers believe clients do not know enough about artwork. A printer may not make a firm bid from your specifications without seeing the final, camera-ready artboards. A printer might prefer to read the artist's instructions before formulating a bid.

A sample printing estimate and quote sheet is presented at the end of this chapter.

BLUELINES

A blueline is a photographic representation of your job that the printer presents as your last chance to check for problems before going to press. At this stage, you should be looking for type broken in the camera process (where page negatives are made), incorrectly placed photographs, and other technical problems. Typos should have been corrected in the artboard or computer disk stage. Read your blueline carefully, check it against your artboards, make sure it is trimmed properly, and mark whatever problems you see on it. The printer will inspect your marks on the blueline and make necessary corrections before printing.

COLOR KEYS

A four-color job will require you to check a color key. Designers often prefer to have their client approve the color key before printing begins. Full-color photographs or artwork are actually made up of four "process" colors: yellow, magenta (red), cyan (blue), and black. The color key shows you the intensity and tone of each color. Individual plastic overlay sheets each carry one of the four colors. Collectively, the four sheets create a full-color photo or graphic. The plastic tends to add a yellow tint, making the colors appear slightly darker than they will print. After you have approved the colors, the printer "steps" the film, which means the printer reproduces it the number of times it takes to fit on a given sheet.

PRESS CHECKING OR PRESS PROOFING

After reviewing a blueline, the printer will make required corrections. Your project will then be ready for printing. You or your designer will want to check the pages as they come off the press. This step of checking (or proofing) the press as it runs is the final opportunity to review and adjust pages. At this stage, only slight alterations can be made.

You cannot press proof a one-color press because after ink is applied, changes or adjustments in color and registration are impossible. It is a common error to assume that a one-color press will be less expensive, but you have to consider the cost of sending a multicolor job through such a press several times. Also, the odds of falling out of registration—creating that out-of-focus, 3-D look that occurs when the color boundaries do not match—increase every time paper travels through the press. Registration problems are exaggerated when you print photographs; they are less conspicuous with type.

Press checks on a four-color press give you options: you can adjust colors by literally turning up the red, turning down the yellow, or turning up the black. After the paper makes one pass through a four-color press, you can see the final full-color version.

Do you need to press check every job? It depends on how precise you are and how much you trust the printer. Small jobs or one-color jobs are often run without a press check. Every new sheet of a press check is slightly different from the generation that preceded it. The printer's price probably includes a certain amount of down time to make these corrections. Printers usually have their own quality control person, but you have every right to protect your investment.

Some clients insist that their graphic designer attend press checks and are willing to pay an extra hourly fee for the service. For a novice communicator, it is worth the price. A designer's trained eye will complement your own and add valuable expertise to the press check process.

Beware of designers who are unfamiliar with the printing process. You should scrutinize their work carefully to be sure that they have not created designs that are overly expensive to print. Equally dangerous are press operators who try to rush you through the press run, thinking your job is finished long before your graphic designer thinks so.

A list of press-proofing pointers appears at the end of this chapter.

WORKS-IN-TURN

One economical printing method is the work-in-turn. This means the printer has to make only one plate to print the front of a sheet of paper and one plate to print the back of the sheet. All the graphic elements fall into the same position, so the printer flips the paper and uses the same plates. Works-in-turn save money and time. Work-in-turn is the most efficient printing technique in any size. An added benefit is that you can check both sides at the same time.

SEPARATIONS, FOLDING, AND BINDING

After you or your photographer, graphic designer, or illustrator supplies photos or artwork, color separations must be made. You may want to control the separation process, but printers are often assigned the task. Many printers send specialized work out to custom separation houses. Special bindery requirements (for custom folds, scoring, and other special services) may also be performed at another vendor's shop. These outside services are often included in a printer's bid.

SENDING A COLOR PHOTO
OR TRANSPARENCY TO A PRINTER

Although you can submit glossy photos, printers prefer working with transparencies (slides). When light is projected through a transparency, the actual and true colors appear, without the inevitable degradation that results from making a print. The transparency is scanned for color and loaded onto a drum, where a computer reads it and divides or separates it into the four process colors. Next, the computer decides what level of each one of those colors is needed to reproduce your finished piece. Because each piece of film is scanned separately, color separations can be very expensive.

The best result occurs if the photo in your finished, printed material appears in a reduced size compared to the original;

enlarging transparencies dilutes color intensity. The larger the transparency, the more accurate the reproduction will be. Shooting down (shrinking) an image for publication concentrates the dot pattern of the photo and gives a crisper reproduction. If possible, use a transparency as your original photo source and reserve color prints for backup.

You should receive a subsequent-generation proof of changes you request on any aspect of a print job—photos, illustrations, color keys, or bluelines. This new proof should show that the work you requested was completed. You will probably be asked to initial the proof to show your approval. Thereafter, the printer is responsible for matching the proof on the press.

ASK YOUR PRINTER

Most printers are helpful and willing to explain the process and answer your questions. They are generous with information and time, so do not hesitate to ask your printer for any information you need. Printers can often arrange a tour of their plant and familiarize you with the equipment and the people with whom you will be working. Some large printers may have brochures explaining the printing process.

Printing is a complicated combination of technology, business, art, and experience. By understanding the procedure, you will also understand why it is so expensive to make changes at the printing stage rather than at the artwork stage. Both you and the printer will save money and time if you understand the process.

Press-Proofing Pointers

Here are solutions to a few common printing problems that you may encounter during a press proof:

Colors out of focus. If colors appear out of focus, check registration. Inspect the dot pattern with a loup or magnifying glass to determine if dots are sharply defined. Blurry dot patterns can develop as the press is adjusted and readjusted. Be sure to check another signature or page. No proof can be matched until registration problems are solved.

Poor quality of four-color pages. If four-color pages seem dull but nearly match the proof, ask the press operator to run the colors stronger while maintaining the same color balance. The page will look flat if colors are light. Increasing the ink volume will result in a brighter reproduction with more contrast and more three-dimensional characteristics. However, be careful not to apply the ink so strongly that the dots begin to merge.

Flat halftones. If black-and-white halftones (photos prepared for printing) appear flat, increase the ink volume for more contrast. If that does not work, check the original film or print for flaws.

Poor Print Quality. If there are excessive interruptions ("hickies") in the print pattern, ask your press person to wash the blanket. This will remove paper particles that cause white spots on the page. If the printed job is unsatisfactory, ask the press operator to check for worn blankets, worn or inferior plates, imperfect ink, or flawed paper. These and other possible problems will require shutting down the press. The earlier these types of problems are discovered, the easier they are to remedy.

Printing estimate and quote sheet

___Quote   Date_____
___Estimate   Purchase order number _____
Job description _____
_____
_____
_____
_____

Printing specifications

Size_____
Pages _____
Paper stock _____
Quantity_____   No overs or unders _____
Number of colors_____
Inks_____
Bleeds _____
Screen tints _____
Halftones_____
Duotones_____
Color separations_____
Folding _____
Scoring_____
Bindery _____
Foil _____
Embossing_____
Die cuts _____
Packing _____
Delivery instructions_____
_____

Notes _____
_____
_____
_____

Client contact _____

Five

Photography

S ometime in your career, and perhaps often, you will hire or work with a professional photographer. To ensure a productive and satisfying relationship, there are several things you should know.

First, you will need to know how to find a pro. You can contact a photographer through recommendations. Communicators often like the tacit assurance of a colleague's endorsement. For the photographer, a personal recommendation may carry an extra degree of motivation. It may also be useful to consult directories, source books, or photographers' representatives.

After finding a professional photographer, you need to understand the hiring process and know what protocol to follow. Look at the photographer's sample book or sample reel. Most professionals will give references gladly if you ask for them, and you should always check those references. You can usually count on honest responses when you do.

The next factors to consider are how to make a deal and how and when to pay. You will also need to know what kind of end product to expect. Will you receive transparencies, (slides), or prints? How many? Will they be in color or in black and white?

You will also need to know what rights you are buying. How may you (and the photographer) use the material? Are photographs to be used in publications only? Or may they also be used in advertisements, promotion materials, ancillary documents such as calendars, marketing items such as T-shirts, broadcast or cable television, etc? If you buy all the rights to a photograph, expect to pay a slightly higher fee because that allows you unlimited use of the work. Discuss the rights up front by describing the exact intended use for the photo.

Most often, photographers are engaged through work-for-hire agreements. That means you, as the employer, own the photo and can use it as you wish. In a work-for-hire situation, the employer is considered the author of the work and is the initial owner of the copyright. Any questions or doubts concerning ownership rights should be submitted to legal counsel. Too often, work-for-hire agreements are sealed only by a handshake. Both parties can avoid problems if the requirements of a specific job are clearly stated and if everyone understands who owns the rights to the work.

Everything is negotiable. Some companies or clients want all the rights. The question then becomes whether the photographer is willing to perform the task under that condition for the amount of money offered, or conversely, whether you are willing to ante up a few more dollars to pay for exclusivity. A sliding pay scale or other negotiated agreement could compensate for possible future windfall earnings from the photo, such as a subsequent poster deal. Under such an agreement, if the image ultimately makes big money, the photographer is entitled to auxiliary payment in addition to the original fee. These considerations not only make an artistic and logistic difference but also affect your overall budget.

YOUR RESPONSIBILITIES
AS A CORPORATE COMMUNICATOR

Working with a photographer is one of the glamorous aspects of a business communications job. However, the success of a photo shoot is equally shared between you and your photographer. On any photo shoot, your responsibility as a corporate communicator is split among several functions.

You Are a Diplomat

During the photo shoot, you are the pivotal person when feathers need to be smoothed or favors must be asked of people while on location. Be prepared for a few groans when equipment or personnel must be unexpectedly requisitioned. Your tact may be tested.

For example, a corporate communicator from a holding corporation accompanied an egocentric but talented photographer on an annual-report photo session to one of the corporation's subsidiaries. The photographer's temperamental attitude was not appreciated by the senior executives who had to sit for portraits. This clash of personalities produced visible tension on the faces of the executives. At separate discreet moments, the corporate communicator apologized to subsidiary management on behalf of the holding corporation and reminded the photographer that he was hired to create useful images, not indifferent ones. Animosities melted and, ultimately, the work produced at that session was used effectively in the annual report. This example shows how important it is never to lose sight of the final product. You must use all your persuasive powers to encourage the best photos your company's or client's money can buy.

You Are Your Company's or Client's Representative

At subsidiaries or at locations where you and your photographer are guests, you must conduct yourself in a way that reflects your corporate culture as practiced in the office.

You Function as Art Director

Work closely with the photographer to best interpret how your company or client is to be represented. In an annual report, for example, you should not photograph a model holding a product that did not sell well. You have to be aware of the relative value of each component of the photograph.

You Are a Consultant

Discuss the shot with your photographer. Explain the goal of the photo and its intended use. Do not assume the photographer knows your product better than you do. Even though the photographer may have more technical knowledge (about lights, lenses, and film) and more expertise in artfully creating a shot, most professionals will listen to your artistic suggestions. One photographer recalls a photo shoot where the assignment was vague: get a good picture of some people for a billboard advertisement. That lack of specificity and direction is unfair to the photographer and indicates that the communicator has not done his or her job.

YOUR RESPONSIBILITIES AS AN EMPLOYER

Your responsibilities as an employer include:

- Communicating your requirements to the photographer with the understanding that making art takes some flexibility by both parties.
- Remembering that the creation process is not free. Everything you ask for has a monetary value.
- Staying involved with the shoot. You should be able to discuss details of the planned sessions and provide feedback.
- Making the photographer's job as easy as possible. That way, the photographer can concentrate on creating the best photo and not be distracted by logistic or political minutiae.
- Protecting, above all, your company's or client's product and image.

INTERVIEWING A PHOTOGRAPHER

Photographers want to work. Therefore, the photographer you contact should approach your initial meeting as if it were a job interview, observing the appropriate standards of dress and demeanor. It is important that both parties maintain an atmosphere of mutual respect.

Smart photographers will also prepare by trying to get an idea of what to present based on your description of the job. They may research what kind of work your company or client does and what you are looking for and then arrange their portfolio accordingly. Photographers experienced in corporate communications work understand that the best picture may not always be chosen for publication or distribution. Many times, a photographer will have to sacrifice an artistic shot in favor of one that you designate as a better reflection of corporate goals.

The photographer you hire should:

- Try to anticipate problems and provide solutions.
- Tell you what is required to get the job done.
- Do the job to your satisfaction.

Topics you should agree upon with the photographer in advance of the shoot include the cancellation policy, the policy regarding delays due to weather or other factors, and what specific circumstances would require a reshoot. Before you agree to hire a photographer, ask yourself: " Given all I know about this photographer, am I convinced that he or she can deliver the product I need?" The photographer will surely be asking, "Given all I know about this project and client, can I deliver the product he or she needs?"

PLANNING A PHOTOGRAPH

When you plan your photo shoot, consider what type of shoot it will be. If it is a portrait, is it to be formal or casual? Where will it be shot, on location or in a studio?

Planning Portraits

In planning portrait shoots, there are a number of sensitive issues to consider. For example, you must decide whether the subject would benefit from a harsh, show-it-all portrait or from a soft look that hides such minor flaws as facial lines and rough skin. Determine if the photo is intended for repro-duction or exhibition. There is intrinsic softening in many print reproduction processes. Portraits diminish in intensity as successive generations or negatives and prints are made.

Should you air-brush a portrait? Consider the ego and clout of your subject as well as the photo's use. You must also consider how best to present a heavy, dewlapped, or physically impaired individual.

What will you suggest for your subject to wear? As a general rule for corporate portraiture, it is advisable that both men and women wear colored or striped shirts or blouses (not white) and that men wear a dark jacket with a contrasting tie.

Should you have a make-up or grooming person present? Although most corporate subjects eschew it, there are few individuals who wouldn't benefit from slight enhancement, especially around the eyes. Make-up is a delicate subject because it involves personal appearance and ego. At least have a comb or brush available. Don't be afraid to pull down the back of a bunched-up suit coat or straighten a crooked tie. Also, if your photo shoot is late in the day, make sure that, if necessary, the subject brings a fresh shirt, tie, and coat and that men have the opportunity to shave. Grooming suggestions should not cause offense. They are important because the image captured on film will be seen by a wide audience. Few subjects argue when you try to make them look their best.

Planning Location Shots

If you choose a location shot, you need to decide whether to visit and explore the site. If possible, both you and the photographer should scout the location. Combining what you know about the company/client, product, and site with the photographer's knowledge about how best to present the subject is a valuable planning step. Having the photographer scout (with you or without you) may result in an extra, but modest, charge. However, the investment buys advanced familiarity with the location and saves time on the day of the shoot.

You will also need to determine who will obtain permission to shoot, permits, release forms, and insurance. This is important where you need the cooperation of some authority for special access or crowd control. Make sure the photographer carries at least $1 million insurance. Everyone appearing in your photo should sign a release form containing language your legal counsel has approved. (See the sample release form at the end of this chapter.)

Determine what technical considerations are necessary for the shoot. Are lighting and power available, or do you need portable sources? Will the wall sockets blow if your photographer plugs in equipment? Do you need special equipment or props?

Always keep some petty cash handy in case you need to buy flowers to fill a frame or a jacket for an unprepared model. You should always be prepared to rent some extra equipment or supply some unforeseen prop during a shoot.

Anticipate whether you will need special personnel. Such people may include underwater camera specialists, a pilot for an aerial shot, equipment operators, technicians, or makeup and grooming people.

Find out whether your crew has to adhere to a dress code. A special event might require a tuxedo. Some corporate environments require photographers to wear suits and ties. Are jeans acceptable?

Carefully plan your budget. How much will you need to spend on permissions; models/talent; expenses such as travel, film, processing, props, donations, messengers, overtime, and incidentals? Do you have to feed your photographer and his or her crew?

DO YOU NEED A PHOTOGRAPHER AT ALL?

The image you want may be available from a **stock photo house**. Stock houses are listed in photo directories and the yellow pages of most phone books. These businesses have catalogs of existing photographs from which you may choose one or several images. You pay on a scale determined by the intended use (brochure, newsletter, magazine, newspaper, broadcast segment, advertisement), position (cover, small illustration), format (black and white, color, stylized), distribution (in-house, direct-mail, trade or consumer publication), and audience (fewer than 1,000, more than 10,000).

GIVING CREDIT

Credit your photographer wherever possible. This gesture serves as extra incentive and motivation for the photographer, and it costs nothing.

Photography release form

I hereby agree that all photographs, negatives, prints, paintings, drawings, sketches, reproductions, and likenesses of any kind made of me or submitted by me to The XYZ Company are and shall remain the property of XYZ, its successors and assigns. I give my irrevocable consent that said works, or any part thereof, may be published, displayed, reproduced, and circulated in any form by XYZ or anyone else authorized by XYZ, with or without my name, for commercial purposes or otherwise, including advertisements in any media and with or without any testimonial copy or other form of advertising or display. I am over 18 years of age.

Date _____

Name _____
(Please print)
Signature _____

Name of minor_____
The above-named is a minor, and as parent or guardian of said minor, I agree to the terms of this release.
Date _____
Signature _____

Six

Videography

C orporate video is a visually captivating and cost-effective communications medium. It is versatile and accommodates many styles: animation, live action, comedy, music, or documentary. Corporate video is most often intended for nonbroadcast purposes and displayed on a VHS- or Beta-format video cassette player/recorder (VCR). Videos are routinely created for:

- Executive messages.
- Product or service promotion.
- Employee orientation.
- Corporate image.
- Sales training and motivation.
- Newsletters.
- Trade show displays.
- Investor, shareholder, employee, or customer relations.
- Educational support.

Corporate video production first blossomed in the automobile industry and large financial institutions. Each of those industries must communicate with offices, branches, and employees around the world. Video became the medium of choice because cassettes or transmissions can be easily delivered to scattered locations and because video has the ability to reach the common comprehension level of demographically diverse audiences.

VIDEO'S BEST USES

There are three areas in which video is best used: training, marketing, and delivering messages.

As a training tool, video is well-suited to enhancing or supplementing information. It is helpful for collateral print materials, such as posters, how-to manuals or facilitator's guides, to complement your video. If training materials have to adhere to a step-by-step process, the related video should match theme and concept but provide a conceptual orientation. Often, print and video are created simultaneously as components of a larger communications package.

The first advantage of video is the consistency of the message. Video's standardized delivery ensures that every viewer will receive the same amount of information, presented exactly as intended.

Second, video greatly facilitates scheduling by allowing employee training sessions or customer viewings to be held at prearranged times (such as at assemblies or trade shows) or at individual convenience (for home or office viewing). Furthermore, an on-screen instructor or host will never be sick or late.

A third advantage of video is its visual impact. Effective videos utilize the many visual tools available to the videographer:

moving camera; talent (actors) in action; eye-pleasing com-
position, lighting, editing, and effects. Add to that the audi-
ence-acceptance factor: almost everyone is accustomed to
viewing images on a television screen—being entertained or
passively receiving information from the ubiquitous glow-
ing box.

It is possible to find a life and value beyond a video's
original purpose. A show created for an employee audience
may be perfectly suitable for business guests, civic groups,
clients, or trade shows.

THE PRODUCTION CONTRACT

A production contract protects both you and the video
provider. Either party may provide or create a contract.
Standard, fill-in-the-blanks agreements exist to cover typical
items such as insurance, employees, liability, ownership of
materials or product, scheduling, deadlines, payment, and
nonperformance.

Usually, the client accepts a bid from the video production
house before signing a contract. The bid results from one or
more brainstorming sessions in which you and the producer
create the format and look of the show. You may receive a
one- or two-page document that:

- Gives the price of producing the show.
- Describes the time and place of the shoot.
- Outlines the number of crewpeople required.
- Recommends tape format, style of the show, voice-
  over, music, and postproduction requirements.

The formal agreement, which follows an accepted bid,
often contains some of these same topics but describes them

in detail. The contract describes payment terms and amounts. Payment is often due in three or four equal installments. The first payment is usually delivered at the beginning of the agreement, before production begins. The second payment is due upon commencement of or completion of principal photography, depending upon the time span involved. The third payment is usually made upon completion of principal photography or commencement of the postproduction process. Final payment is made upon delivery of the master tape.

The contract also specifies the performance timeframe and production terms such as approvals, submission of background documents or other necessary material, and cancellation policy.

Another issue addressed in the agreement is ownership of the product. As the client of a video production house, you usually own the field tapes, the various generations used in editing, and the master tape—all prints and originals. Owning the tape ensures your rights to future use. The disadvantage of ownership is storing all the tape boxes.

The contract also assigns responsibility for loss, damage, or defects to the product and responsibility for equipment. Who procures, maintains, operates, returns, rents, leases, buys, or borrows the gear? Customarily, the video service provider handles equipment details. Make sure that your producer has at least a $1 million liability insurance policy.

The production contract may address issues of confidentiality. The video service provider and his or her employees may be required to refrain from discussing executive messages, new products, site specification, or proprietary information discovered during production.

Under a contract's "pay or play" clause, you, as the client, will be obligated to pay for the video whether or not you use it. This is akin to the graphic designer's kill fee clause described in chapter five.

PRODUCTION PLANNING

There are three main phases involved in producing a corporate video: preproduction, production, and postproduction. A complete list of the tasks appears in the chronology of a video project at the end of this chapter.

Preproduction

Preproduction is the period of planning meetings in which you and your video production staff brainstorm ideas; write the script; scout locations; discuss the shoot; create the show's style; and establish the schedule, dates, and deadlines.

During preproduction, you should answer a wide range of questions. You must decide how early in the planning stages to engage a video production house. Do you have sufficient video experience among your colleagues or do you need assistance from the beginning? You must also determine the topic, the audience, and the purpose of the show. What reaction do you want from the target audience after viewing the program?

It is important to consider the ultimate distribution and viewing environment. Will it be viewed in a big theater that requires video projection equipment or in a meeting room? Will elements of the program be mixed in a multimedia presentation? Will the audience be moving, as at a trade show, or will it be seated? Will the audience be required to watch, or will it view the program voluntarily?

You need to decide who will write the script. You or your video service provider may do the writing, or you may collaborate. You may also engage some other in-house source or a freelance writer.

During preproduction you must plan the budget. The information you compile on the video budget planning sheet at the end of this chapter will help you determine a production budget figure. Each video you plan has its own characteristics. You may not need every category suggested on the planning sheet, or you may have special requirements to add.

Video producers would prefer to know how much money you have to spend as early in your relationship as possible. It helps them plan, especially for postproduction possibilities. Of course, you do not have to divulge an exact figure. Keep in mind, however, that video productions can cost as much as you are able to spend. Beware that the money you spend is evident on the screen and does not disappear in expense account charges or excessive operations charges for security, secretarial services, or catering, for example. Other budget-related considerations include whether to use professional talent (actors) or employees and whether any special equipment or props are required.

Determine during preproduction who has final script approval. What is the process for approval? Who is responsible for the scope and accuracy of the tape? Although you contract with the video provider, it is your boss or possibly his or her boss who will make the final decision about content. Ideally, the ultimate decision maker should be involved and available.

During preproduction you should look for exciting information about the subject of your show. Startling facts or interesting anecdotes will help the script writer and director.

The video client requirement and profile form at the end of this chapter is a tool that your producer might use when planning a video project. It summarizes the important facts he or she will need to know.

Production

The video is shot during the production phase. Like preproduction, production entails a range of questions:

- Who obtains the equipment? Does your production house have the necessary equipment, or does it need to rent?

- What is the production schedule? Your video producer can estimate whether your idea will take two days or two weeks to shoot.

- Are there any special production considerations? Are special technical skills, extra crew, or added security precautions required?

Postproduction

After videography has been completed, postproduction begins. In postproduction the unedited tape is assembled for editing. Relevant questions to consider include:

- What effects would you like? Animation? Blue screen?

- Are postproduction charges included in the price you were quoted? Who reserves editing time?

- Do you want music or sound effects? Where do you obtain them? How do you pay for them?

THE VIDEO PRODUCTION PROCESS

Once production planning and shooting the video have been completed, final assembly begins.

The **field tapes** (the body of video shot) must be transferred to 3/4-inch tape or VHS (1/2-inch) tape so that both you and the video service provider can see them easily.

Next, a **window-dub time code** is applied so that the time code (hours, minutes, seconds, and frames) is "burned" into the tape. The time code does not appear in the picture because it resides on the tape's black bar, out of viewing range. Every frame has an individual time code number.

There are two levels of completion in video production: off-line editing and on-line editing.

Off-Line Editing

Unlike film editing, where actual cuts occur, window-dubbed tapes are edited electronically. Images are transferred from one machine to another. An off-line edit is equivalent to a rough cut of a film—all the images appear in proper sequence, give or take a few frames.

Next, a **guide track** of the audio is applied if a voice-over is planned. Someone reads the script over the assembled images to check the pacing and sequence of the show. The guide track is applied to the off-line edited version of the visuals.

You and your producer will review the rough version of the show on VHS or 3/4-inch tape. The temptation is to add as much as possible on screen. Resist this impulse and keep it simple. Corporate communications are intended first to inform, then to entertain. Your producer should counsel you and, regardless of what he or she thinks of your decision, do as you request. The producer will make revisions in the tape. It may take two or three further off-line edit sessions to make the changes work properly. This is the time to make substantive changes. After the off-line portion of the production sequence, changes become costly in time and money. After you indicate satisfaction with the rough version of the show, the producer may ask you to sign an approval form.

Finally, you will plan where the visual effects will occur in the show, which effects to use, which music to use, and other details that are applied during on-line editing.

On-Line Editing

The on-line editing session polishes the rough version of the show. At this time, special effects, music, the voice-over narration, and other details are applied.

On-line editing charges begin at several hundred dollars an hour. Your time should be spent honing the show, not rearranging its flow. Changing an effect (say from a tumbling image to a spinning image) is expensive and time-consuming. It may also require an entire new 1-inch master tape. Replacing one shot with another is not as big a problem, but it will slow the on-line process.

Costly changes are another reason you need to approve the off-line version of your show. You do not want to see your show for the first time at the on-line session. Make sure your contract provides off-line approval.

VARIETIES OF VIDEOTAPE

Commonly, corporate video utilizes three videotape sizes. The familiar 1/2-inch tape is the most convenient and accepted format for viewing and distribution. The next step up is 3/4-inch tape, which is found in many professional environments such as broadcast newsrooms. Beyond that is 1-inch tape, which is used more often in editing and studio recording than in location shooting. Many field producers now use the Betacam format, which combines the technical superiority of 1-inch with the mobile convenience of smaller-format tapes.

You can also shoot on film, but you will need a bigger budget. Shooting on film, transferring to videotape and applying postproduction shine can increase costs by 25 to 40 percent. This is due to the fact that a high-quality format is necessary—at least 3/4-inch tape but ideally Betacam. That extra expense provides the soft, rich, deep image and saturation of color associated with film. Video is harsh.

Resist the temptation to shoot your company's or client's video on your Camcorder. Even though the tape may look acceptable when played on the home or office VCR, you are only half done. The tape has to be edited.

If you have ever made a copy of a VHS tape, you know it looks fuzzier than the original. That problem grows exponentially as subsequent copies are made each time an edit is required. By the second or third generation, the on-screen image is indistinct and virtually unwatchable.

VISUAL EFFECTS

One of corporate video's ever-present challenges is to make an unattractive business venue (oil fields, shipyards, refineries, manufacturing plants, industrial equipment) or a difficult subject (nervous executives) look visually interesting and appealing to an audience.

The visual effects audiences take for granted—such as fades, dissolves, flying or spinning images—cost extra, and the costs mount quickly. Make sure your video producer informs you about the individual charges of every on-screen spin, twirl, fold, and bend. Think of special graphic effects as a la carte items on the video production menu. Special effects create visual excitement, but you have to be mindful of their effect on your budget.

Unusual visual effects such as animation and computer graphics are especially expensive—you pay a premium for them. Even though special effects and animation take longer to create than most video images, the investment in time is often worth the expense. These effects add sparkle to a video through eye-arresting images. Quick cuts and fast-moving pictures call a viewer's attention to the screen. Animation can be effectively used to explain processes and illustrate functions. For example, animation can graphically demonstrate to an audience the function or operation of technical equipment or logically explain activities that cannot be seen with the naked eye, such as the flow of air through a turbine engine. Without question, visual effects and animation appeal to a demographically varied audience. Used strategically, these video techniques are among the most potent available to a professional communicator.

MUSIC

Music can make an otherwise uninspiring video subject pleasing and accessible. It announces the tone of the presentation and sets the mood for a specific scene. Audiences immediately associate with popular, recognizable tunes. Familiar melodies soften an audience and help transmit the message.

How is music obtained? Ask your producer. There are several sources: music libraries, professional recordings, and original music.

If your show will be seen by the public, then you must secure rights to copyrighted music. Virtually all popular recordings have copyright protection. If the audience is exclusively internal, then you might approach music licenses

casually. Beware—you will be liable for any copyright in-
fringements because you own the show.

When you buy from a music library, you pay a licensing fee
based on the length of the piece and its intended use (Will it be
broadcast? On radio? AM or FM? Television? VHF or UHF?
What market or markets? Cablecast? When? How many times?
Commercial recording? Advertisement? In-house use?). The
danger of using music from a library is that other people may
have already used the music you have chosen.

One corporate communicator on the West Coast chose an
up-tempo piece of music from a music library to enhance a
corporate image show targeted primarily for East Coast securities analysts. During the show, he was unhappy to hear people
snickering where no laugh was intended. After the show, he
found out that the music he chose was associated with Sam the
Discount Butcher, a low-budget, late-night television adver-
tiser on the East Coast. Apparently Sam had set words to this
particular piece of music that were famous for their silliness. Of
course, the business communicator unintentionally broke the
mood of his show for that audience.

ORDERING COPIES

The last step in the production cycle is ordering the number
of duplicates, boxes, and labels you want. This may include
the services of a duplication house for copies and a graphic
designer for custom-made labels.

KEEP IT MOVING

Video is a dynamic medium. Moving images are its essence and
power. Talking heads (people on screen who only talk to the
camera and never move) will neither inform nor entertain.

Equally deadly is the seated executive—just an individual at a desk, without proper lighting, obviously uncomfortable on camera. It is universally agreed that the least effective video presentations feature executives or employees on camera for long periods of time.

Some business video producers think talking heads are fine. One or two suited figures on screen convey the dignity and credibility associated with news anchorpeople. Also, this kind of show is inexpensive to produce. Even though talking heads are required occasionally, use them sparingly—they are dull.

Other video writers and producers insist that executives have to entertain the viewer. The answer depends on the situation, on the company, and the viewing audience.

COST

Video producers complain that most business communicators do not fully understand all the elements that go into a production. Conversely, corporate clients are often shocked to read the grand total at the bottom of their video service supplier's invoice. Video costs vary for several reasons:

- Competition. Are there several video production houses in your city vying for your business?
- Production decisions. The answers to questions discussed in the "Production Planning" section of this chapter will affect your final cost.
- Postproduction decisions. Every eye-catching special effect you put on screen has a dollar value. Ask your producer.

USE YOUR JUDGMENT

The market is full of talented video producers, writers, and videographers. You must find a talented one with whom you can work harmoniously and who has worked successfully within the corporate environment. Your video team should be as familiar with corporate protocol as it is with production techniques.

Chronology of a Video Project

(1) Client decides to produce a video program.

(2) Client reviews sample reels submitted by prospective video producers.

(3) Client chooses video producer.

(4) Client and video producer agree to terms.

(5) Client and video producer discuss the show they will produce.

(6) Client pays one third of video production fee.

(7) Client and video producer agree on script.

(8) Video producer gathers crew, begins shooting.

(9) Client makes second of three payments.

(10) Client attends shooting to ensure integrity of message.

(11) After shooting, video producer prepares off-line edit.

(12) Client approves off-line edit or suggests changes.

(13) Video producer prepares on-line edit, which includes visual effects, music, titles, etc.

(14) Video producer presents master tape to client.

(15) Client makes final payment to video producer.

(16) Client orders copies made from master tape.

(17) Client distributes tapes.

Video budget planning sheet

Date _____

Project title _____

Producer _____

Address _____

Telephone _____

Facsimile _____

Project deadline date _____

Budget guideline

	Rate	Day/hour	Total
Producer	____.__	× _____	____.__
Director	____.__	× _____	____.__
Storyboard artist	____.__	× _____	____.__
Camera operator	____.__	× _____	____.__
Videotape	____.__	× _____	____.__
Sound mixer	____.__	× _____	____.__
Boom operator	____.__	× _____	____.__
Radio microphones	____.__	× _____	____.__
Lighting technician	____.__	× _____	____.__
Talent/actor(s)	____.__	× _____	____.__
	____.__	× _____	____.__
	____.__	× _____	____.__
	____.__	× _____	____.__
Extras	____.__	× _____	____.__
Makeup/hair artist	____.__	× _____	____.__
Catering	____.__	× _____	____.__
Props	____.__	× _____	____.__
Special camera operator	____.__	× _____	____.__
Insurance	____.__	× _____	____.__
Scouting costs	____.__	× _____	____.__
Travel and living	____.__	× _____	____.__

Vehicle rentals	_____.___ × _____	_____.___
Stage rental	_____.___ × _____	_____.___
Location rental	_____.___ × _____	_____.___
Permits	_____.___ × _____	_____.___
Doctor/nurse	_____.___ × _____	_____.___
Police/guards	_____.___ × _____	_____.___
Firefighters	_____.___ × _____	_____.___
Special equipment	_____.___ × _____	_____.___
Steadicam	_____.___ × _____	_____.___
Wind machine	_____.___ × _____	_____.___
TelePromptR unit	_____.___ × _____	_____.___
Underwater gear	_____.___ × _____	_____.___
Walkie-talkies	_____.___ × _____	_____.___
Bullhorn	_____.___ × _____	_____.___
Batteries/power	_____.___ × _____	_____.___
Postproduction	_____.___ × _____	_____.___
On-line edit bay	_____.___ × _____	_____.___
Time code copies	_____.___ × _____	_____.___
Videotape editor	_____.___ × _____	_____.___
Visual effects	_____.___ × _____	_____.___
Music	_____.___ × _____	_____.___
Composer	_____.___ × _____	_____.___
Studio time	_____.___ × _____	_____.___
Musicians/singers	_____.___ × _____	_____.___
Copyrights	_____.___ × _____	_____.___
TOTAL		_____.___
Taxes		_____.___
GRAND TOTAL		_____.___

Video client requirement and profile form

Date _____

Prepared by _____

Project title _____

Client/company _____

Contact/department_____

Client address_____
_____

Telephone _____

Program topic_____

Purpose _____
_____

Target audience _____
_____

Desired reaction of audience after viewing program _____
_____
_____
_____

Final distribution and viewing environment _____
_____
_____
_____

Projected production schedule _____
_____

Projected production budget_____
_____

Special production considerations _____
_____

Crew _____
_____
_____
_____

Locations_____
_____
_____

Talent _____

_____

_____

_____

_____

Equipment_____

_____

Effects _____

_____

_____

Other _____

_____

_____

Individuals responsible for scope and accuracy of content
Name   *Title*   *Phone*

_____

_____

_____

_____

_____

_____

Existing information on program topic _____

_____

_____

Script approval process_____

_____

_____

Final program approval _____

_____

_____

_____

Seven

Events

E very corporate event has its own goal. There is no such thing as a business event with no reason for being. Many corporations now respect and value the importance of special events. Organizations commonly dedicate staff, entire departments, or consultants exclusively to special projects and events.

The first step for any successful event is deciding its objective. Is it intended to:

- Cultivate clients?
- Thank employees?
- Introduce a new product or venue?
- Educate people?

Once the purpose is defined, you can decide how to achieve the desired goal.

Keep closely associated with the event and resist the temptation to dump the planning and execution into the lap of secretary, colleague, or consultant. You must monitor everyone's participation.

An outstanding event need not be expensive or resort to flashy tricks. Guests appreciate a well-run event—primarily because they go to so many poorly planned ones. Misplaced reservations, misspelled or missing name tags, instructions to sit at an already full table, inedible food, or a boring speaker add up to a waste of time and resources.

PREPARING FOR THE EVENT

Several simple factors contribute to a successful event.

Written Programs and Invitations

Establish a theme for the event and develop and invitation for it. The theme should appear consistently on every piece of material associated with that event: the invitation, correspondence accompanying the invitation, the art, the printed program, the menu card, linens, decorations, and flowers.

The unifying graphics should also take into consideration the colors to be used at the event and the tone or atmosphere you want to create. Will this be a classy, elegant affair or is it a fun, festive occasion? The invitation should cue the guests to the tenor of the event. An engraved card with tissue paper signals an elegant event. A giant invitation with colored calligraphy means fun. Try to link the event and the venue to the invitation. If the venue is a museum, print your invitation on a museum gift shop card.

Even though the invitation may be addressed to a top executive, he or she rarely sees this kind of mail. CEOs don't usually open their own mail, their secretaries do, and those are the people your invitation must impress. Because your envelope is just one item in a ceiling-high stack of mail the secretary must sort, if it is not eye-catching it will go in the wastebasket. The secretary will put your invitation or letter at the top of the CEO's pile only if he or she sees an important signature on it or is impressed with its look.

An invitation garners better response than does a letter. Form letters, photocopied letters, and letters without a big-name signature never work.

Food

Food arrangements need supreme attention, whether you are offering fruit and cheese or a sit-down dinner. Do not leave food selection to a hotel or caterer.

Insist on a tasting. Go privately to the hotel in which your event is scheduled, sit with the catering manager, and select either from their menu or from the selection you propose. A caterer may be able to arrange a tasting or send samples. If he or she can't do that, discuss the meal in detail. A tasting session can help avoid:

- The unnecessarily complicated production of an arty chef.
- Poor presentation.
- Clashes of flavors or styles.
- Unhappy guests who have been served portions so small that half the plate was bare.

Some things are bound to change between planning and presentation—slight variations will occur. But if you tasted poached pear in raspberry sauce at the planning stage and find chocolate mousse at your event, that is a sufficient reason to state your displeasure.

Don't let catering directors intimidate you. If you don't know about food, ask. If you don't know about wine, ask. If you don't understand a term, ask.

Don't accept a prescribed list of menus in all situations. Ask if they can be flexible. Keep in mind that you are the caterer's client. In fact, you potentially represent several hundred clients. Each of your guests may want to use the same venue or caterer if they liked the event. You can use that bargaining power to ask for—and get—what you want. Most caterers and hotels will make every effort to satisfy your requests.

If a service provider will not give you adequate attention because of the small size of your group, go elsewhere. Small meetings may be the most powerful, involving CEOs, senior executives, and other high-profile individuals who may, in turn, use the same facilities.

For a buffet offering, coordinate the supply of food with your caterer. You are paying for a specific amount of food, but you probably don't want it all presented at one time because the food display will be picked over in 20 minutes. A caterer should be instructed to put out food gradually and have a sufficient number of staff people to monitor food supplies.

If possible, donate surplus food to established charities. Many city ordinances restrict reusing food after it has been offered for public consumption, but it may be possible to deliver to regional food banks unserved leftovers from the kitchen.

Plan your event as if you were a guest. Think of yourself trying to converse with a senior executive while your mouth is full. Don't order a sloppy soup—think of all those silk ties and cocktail dresses that will need dry-cleaning. Don't order food that guests have to fight to eat, such as meat on a bone or certain finger foods. Don't order food on sticks, such as shishkabob. Try to choose satisfying menu selections that can be consumed gracefully.

Menu Cards

A menu card describes each course of the menu and the wine selection. A simple dinner can become an elegant one by adding a menu card at each place setting. Guests appreciate them and may keep them as souvenirs of the event. Menu cards can be formatted on a personal computer. With the help of a few type fonts and a laser printer, you can create a stylish ambience at low cost.

If you produce a menu card, make sure nothing changes before the event. If your menu card describes a salad with vinaigrette and crumbled blue cheese, but the chef is too lazy to crumble blue cheese over it before serving, be prepared for someone to announce loudly, "I don't see any crumbled blue cheese on my salad." Inform the caterer, chef, or hotel that you are using a menu card. Show them the draft, agree on wording and content, and give them one of the final cards to hang in the kitchen.

Program Card or Agenda

You may want to generate a program card that carries details of the entire event. This is especially useful for multifaceted, lengthy events: a meal, a host welcoming the attendees, introduction of a guest speaker, and an adjournment. Just like the menu card, a program card is simple, easy to create, and inexpensive, but it serves as a helpful guide for guests and as a welcome souvenir. It may also save people from leaving early.

Guests retain unpleasant memories of an event that takes too long. Promise your guests from the beginning what time you will adjourn and stick to that time even if it means dropping someone from the agenda. Instruct your speakers to adhere to a prearranged amount of time.

Flowers

Always inspect a sample of the floral arrangements, just as you taste the food. If you tell the florist what kind of event is planned and the amount you can spend, he or she should be able to provide a free sample. A small florist may not be able to supply a free arrangement, and in that case, offer to pay for it. It is worth every penny to get a sample. The lavish flora described in telephone conversations rarely materialize in reality.

Avoid carnations and daisies. Florists often use them as fillers, but they look cheap. Some event planners have a rule against those two flowers—greenery or a few exotic blossoms are more dramatic and aesthetically appealing.

Make sure your guests can see each other across the table. Centerpieces should be kept low, and tall arrangements should have thin stems. After paying good cash for centerpieces, you don't want guests to move them off the table because they can't see over or through them.

Offer the flowers to your guests by having your host announce at the end of the event that the flowers may be taken. If you don't give them to guests, send them to a hospital or present them to the staff (especially the volunteers) who worked at the event. Alert the receiving institution in advance that you want to donate flowers on a specific day.

THE PROGRAM

When you think about the program, ask yourself, "What is the intent of the evening?" Make sure your speaker's remarks clearly reflect your goal and intent. Many CEOs and executives can't speak comfortably and extemporaneously, so you may have to write remarks for them.

Have your speaker begin his or her remarks at a time during the event when you have peak attendance. Don't start before the greatest number of people have arrived and don't wait too long. Six people listening to the chairman of the board is not a success. If you have a reception from 6:00 to 7:30 P.M., schedule the speaker around 6:30 or 6:45 P.M. Again, think of yourself as a guest. You don't want to be the first arrival at a cocktail reception, so you show up a little late.

At a dinner, your program can begin at dessert time. Let your guests enjoy their food. Never rush the meal. Never whisk plates away from guests with forks in their hands. Leave enough time for the meal. Hotel staff may promise that they can serve a four-course meal in 45 minutes or an hour, but the potential is great for underestimating the actual time required. If you must present a four-course meal in an hour, hire extra serving people. Assign one server per table. Although most hotels don't use that many serving people, they can certainly assign them if you pay for the extra help.

Make sure your guests aren't rushed and your program isn't hurried. Guests should enjoy themselves and their food. By the time coffee and dessert are served, your speakers are ready to begin.

Servers should not linger in the dining area after the program has begun. It is better for guests to wait for another cup of coffee than for dishes to clatter and servers to weave between tables after the first speaker stands up. Theoretically, the speaker has the group's attention and should not be forced to compete with housekeeping chores.

INTRODUCTIONS AT THE EVENT

Any member of your company or client's staff should be considered a host for the event and be encouraged to make introductions. This is not pushy, it is courteous. When name tags are used, introductions are easier. At an elegant event, name tags are out of place. Recruit executives as roving hosts to mingle with guests. Provide a list of who is attending. When key people enter, introduce them to the host if you don't have a receiving line. The guest will be flattered to be introduced and relieved to have the conversation formally initiated. If you are timid about introducing guests, executives in your organization may miss the opportunity to meet big clients who attend.

Seating charts are important for the same reason. If you know where every important person is located, you can send your senior executives around to visit tables.

GUEST SPEAKERS

Preplanned programs are important. You must prepare (and rehearse) the content of your event. Speakers, even speakers from within your organization, need to prepare. More often than not, they will need your assistance as well. Essentially, you must babysit your guest speaker from confirmation of the date to the end of his or her speech. If you don't keep in close contact with your speakers, you may end up with the speeches they want and not the speeches you want them to give. You want to maintain control so *your* program does not become *their* program.

Every speaker should receive a copy of the event's agenda. You must explain every detail to your guest speakers for two reasons. First, it establishes your role as the pivotal event person, and second, it is a courtesy to provide your principal guests the basic information they need:

- Time limitations.
- Topics of discussion.
- Other guests attending.
- Background material on your company or client.
- The goal of the meeting.

This is particularly true for outside speakers and panel discussion participants. It is unfair to complain about poor speeches if you have not informed your speakers sufficiently.

If you can't get an advance copy of your guest's speech, get an outline. Ask outside speakers what they are going to talk about so you can inform those within your organization.

Follow your speakers through your event. Insist on having a car pick them up at the airport and bring them to your location. This is a flattering courtesy and it ensures that your guest will arrive on time. Provide return transportation as well.

Speakers' Agencies or Privately Invited Speakers

Many outside speakers come from personal or professional contacts with your board of directors or senior executive staff. A letter from an associate or acquaintance is often more productive than engaging a speaker through an agency. A speaker may deal with you directly if he or she knows your organization or is intrigued by the topic. Others insist you go through their agencies.

Even if you are operating on a tight budget, do not automatically cross off a big-name speaker. There are people who purposely make themselves available for speaking engagements. Do not assume an honorarium is necessary, especially if you are working without a booking agency. You may be able to entice a well-known speaker with a provocative idea or a desirable audience. Don't forget that your event provides the speaker with visibility, attention, possible press coverage, and a forum from which to deliver his or her message. You might provide the audience your speaker has never reached before. Actually, you are doing your speaker a favor, not the other way around.

If you cannot sign a speaker without promising an honorarium (or a contribution to his or her charity or cause), then do it. If you must go through an agency, so be it.

Even if you avoid a speaker's fee, some money will have to be spent. Travel expenses (airfare/trainfare, hotel, and meals) are often paid by the host organization. As a courtesy, offer to pay for your speaker's spouse to accompany him or her. If it is a business trip, the principal may decline, but be prepared to provide that service.

Your company or client may want a specific, famous, or controversial speaker. If so, be prepared to deal with that person's requests and demands. These people can cost more than a speaker's fee. Their traveling entourage must also be accommodated. The principal may require the hotel's presidential suite. The group may automatically dine in your city's most expensive restaurants. These ancillary expenses must be considered in your budget.

It is especially important to know the number of people accompanying a foreign guest—he or she is certainly not going to show up alone. Expect a press person, a speech writer, and a spouse to attend. One West Coast corporation was pleased that a former prime minister of Japan agreed to speak at a conference for no fee. He arrived, however, with 25 people in tow. Hotel expenses (at approximately $3,000 a night for the former prime minister's suite alone) surpassed whatever his speaking fee could have been.

The terms of agreement between you and the speaker are, of course, negotiable. In some cases, you have to say no and refuse to pay for extreme demands. You risk losing a big speaker, but you save yourself (and your company or client) money and headaches. Make sure the senior executives overseeing your event know that these things are all variable. Ask them if they are willing to pay for extras if need be.

Ask whether a speaker is traveling solely for your event or whether he or she plans other appearances. A speaker traveling any distance for your event may be tempted to fill up his or her schedule and collect multiple fees. In such cases, you should be able to pay on a prorated basis for your event only. You could offer to pay for their hotel the night of your engagement only and avoid several extra days' worth of charges. You may be able to share expenses with another group.

Before engaging a speaker, ask; "Who is coming with you?" and " Do you need a car?"

If the principal does not give you details, get them from his or her assistant. This will avoid unpleasant and costly surprises.

Panels, Hosts, and Moderators

Ask for provocative topics, especially in a panel discussion. Avoid a panel of "talking heads" discussing aspects of your business. Make sure your panel moderator knows to limit a panel speaker's initial remarks to 5 or 10 minutes. Always allow for questions and answers, because this is the time the audience comes alive.

The most important person on a panel is the moderator. Do not underestimate the usefulness of the position by assigning the responsibility to an executive who will remain passive on the dais and not say a word. The moderator must ask probing questions, keep people on track, follow up on interesting topics, and watch the clock. He or she should be able to guide the question-and-answer session as well as provide a cogent summary of the entire discussion. The moderator should be given a biography of every speaker and should know each speaker's topic. Conversely, your speakers should know who the moderator is.

The designated host should also have a biography of everyone he or she will introduce. You may want to write the introduction and give it to the host. There is a remote possibility that a guest speaker will provide his or her own prepared introduction. You are not obliged to use that material, but you may incorporate some of it into your version of the introduction.

MANAGING THE EVENT

Even though special events are festive, they should be considered serious pieces of business. Professional communicators are responsible for entertaining guests and, in turn, participating in the development of business. Your events are designed to guide people to take a desired course of action. Your guests, however, should never know that they are being manipulated. They should leave feeling entertained, invigorated, or educated.

As the event planner, you should never be so bogged down in one aspect of the event that you can't float around to see all the activities. Assign specific responsibilities to your staff. Even though you are the master planner—the producer—you can't do everything. Use a checklist like the one at the end of this chapter in the early stages of planning. It will define responsibilities and spread the workload evenly.

Always treat your staff courteously. Don't make them work the entire event. Allow breaks for food and a chance to see the festivities. Offer the staff the flower arrangements (if possible) and give them a gift if one is given to guests. If it is not appropriate for the staff to be seated at guest tables during a sit-down dinner, have the caterer provide food for them in another room, but do not send them home hungry.

Just because you use volunteers, does not mean you must settle for just anybody. Use staff who understand that they represent the company. A person handing out name tags is as much a representative of your company or client as is the chairman who makes a 20-minute speech. If the person giving name tags is rude or busy eating or drinking at the check-in desk, the spirit and tenor of the event are damaged.

Guests should never be aware of any behind-the-scenes machinations. For instance, never let them see you argue with the caterer if you *must* argue. You should never lose your cool, especially in the public areas of an event.

The following pages carry samples of documents you may find helpful for the event-planning process. Modify them to suit your specific requirements. The event plan, usually created after arrangements have been made but before the event, describes timing and logistics. Every participant—vendors, volunteers, hosts, speakers, and planners—should receive a copy. This sample was created for a dinner celebrating the opening of a new manufacturing plant. The key contact list shows the main service providers you have engaged. The responsibilities and assignments sheet shows individual staff members' tasks and their progress.

Event Plan

Dinner and dedication of new manufacturing facility

Date _____

Venue site _____

6:30 P.M.   Cocktail reception begins. As guests enter the parking lot off A Street, they will have their choice of valet or self-parking. A security officer will be on duty in the parking lot all evening.

Signs on the front of the plant will be lit so that they are visible to guests from the street. Interior and exterior lighting will be done by ABC Associates, who will handle all lighting arrangements for the entire dinner.

As guests enter the main doors (which are automatic to facilitate handicap access), they will see two registration tables: A–K on one side and L–Z on the other. Registration will be supervised by a secretarial support staff member from the company. Coats can be checked at the desk, where guests will receive a claim ticket. A staff person will deliver coats to the designated office for storage. A security person will be stationed in the area all evening. At the end of the event, coat racks will be wheeled out into the lobby in order to facilitate collection of coats.

After registering, guests will be given a seat assignment card and will then proceed into the lobby area for cocktails. Catering for the evening will be handled by XYZ Catering. Two eight-foot bars will be set up in the lobby—one against the elevator bank and one alongside the north wall. Wine and hors d'oeuvres will be passed from trays. We will serve only cold hors d'oeuvres to comply with the city fire department's no-cooking rule in the building. The offices adjacent to the lobby will be used by the caterer for food preparation and for a service bar.

7:00 P.M. The dedication ceremony begins. There will be a lectern and microphone set up next to where the dedication block will be placed. The chairman will call people to attention, introduce himself, and make two minutes of remarks. He will then introduce the mayor, who will speak for two minutes. The chairman will speak again for about five minutes about the importance of the new plant.

He will remind guests of the impending tours. He will read the inscription of the plaque, acknowledge those persons whose name is on the dedication block and introduce two members of the plant's staff who will put the dedication block into place. This will end the dedication ceremony.

7:15 P.M. (approximately). Tours begin. One or two tours will be available at 6:30 P.M. in case the lobby becomes too crowded. Nineteen guides will bring groups of 10 to 12 guests at a time on 20-minute tours of the plant. Tours will end on the main manufacturing floor where the dinner will be served. Two concurrent tour routes have been mapped.

7:45 P.M. Guests will have arrived on the main manufacturing floor for the start of dinner. As guests arrive and throughout dinner, a harpist will play in this area. In order to hasten guests taking their seats, the chairman will proceed to the lectern and welcome everyone, introduce the board of directors in attendance, ask that all guests be seated, and announce that no smoking is permitted in the facility.

There will be 40 tables (66-inch rounds) set up, five rows with 8 tables per row. Tables will be covered with ivory underlays that drop to the floor, peach overlays, and ivory napkins. Ivory china will be used. Chiavari chairs with ivory cushions will surround each table.

Floral centerpieces will be on stands, reaching a height of about 60 inches off the table. There will be no votive candles. Fire regulations prohibit other greenery around the periphery of the room.

At each place setting, there will be an ivory program for each guest, highlighting the dinner schedule and menu. Also, there will be a wrapped box containing a commemorative lapel pin. On each chair will be a wrapped copy of our company's history. These will be wrapped in ivory paper topped with a bow to match the decor.

The caterer will prepare food out of sight of the guests. The dinner includes:

Red pepper soup with cheese pastry twists
Au Bon Climat
1988 Santa Barbara County Chardonnay

Fresh poached salmon with sorrel butter
Gratin dauphinas
Orange-glazed baby steamed carrots
Asparagus tips sauté *al dente*
Edna Valley 1985 *pinot noir*

European seven-lettuce and citrus salad
Lime dressing
Dill French toast

Dutch chocolate *Creme Anglaise* with fresh berries

Coffee and tea

Fish was chosen as an entreé because the event was held during Lent—otherwise we would have offered a choice. The caterer felt two entrees were too difficult to prepare in portable kitchen conditions.

There will be lights hung from the ceiling, with pin spot lighting on each table. Primary lighting will be designed to complement the table settings. All lighting equipment will have been set up on the previous day.

9:15 P.M. (approximately). Dinner service is completed. The chairman returns to the lectern and, after brief remarks, introduces the guest speaker who will speak for 15 to 20 minutes.

9:45 P.M. The chairman will thank everyone for attending and adjourn the dinner. Guests will leave. There will be guides and staff along the exit route, and a staff person in the lobby will have rolled the coat racks out.

10 P.M. Clean-up begins.

Key contact list

Event name_____

Date _____

Location_____

Time _____

Speaker(s) _____

_____

_____

Speaker's business telephone number(s)   _____

_____

_____

Speaker's home telephone number(s)   _____

_____

_____

Speaker's local accommodations _____

_____

_____

Caterer_____

_____

_____

Rental company _____

_____

_____

Florist_____

_____

Music _____

_____

Transportation _____

_____

Audiovisual/lighting _____

_____

Staff/assignments _____

_____

_____

Other _____

_____

Responsibilities and assignments sheet

Event name _____

Event date _____

Location _____

Time _____

Letters of invitation

Staff_____

Status _____ Date _____

Note _____

Invitation list

Staff_____

Status _____ Date _____

Note _____

Printing (letters, RSVP cards, envelopes, programs, menu cards):

Staff_____

Status _____ Date _____

Note _____

Response tally

Staff_____

Status _____ Date _____

Note _____

Catering contact

Staff_____

Status _____ Date _____

Note _____

Equipment rental contact

Staff_____

Status _____ Date _____

Note _____

Venue details

Audiovisual equipment (slides, videotape, film, overhead transparencies, TV monitors, microphones, screens)

Staff_____

Status _____ Date _____

Note _____

Guest tours
Staff _____
Status _____ Date_____
Note _____
Inspections, permits
Staff _____
Status _____ Date_____
Note _____
Insurance
Staff _____
Status _____ Date_____
Note _____

Guest details
Gifts
Staff _____
Status _____ Date_____
Note _____
Meeting materials (newspapers, notepads, pens, pencils, hand-outs)
Staff _____
Status _____ Date_____
Note _____

Program
Welcoming remarks
Staff _____
Status _____ Date_____
Note _____
Luncheon/dinner remarks
Staff _____
Status _____ Date_____
Note _____
Special remarks
Staff _____
Status _____ Date_____
Note _____

Speaker coordination
Speaker(s) _____
Telephone number(s)_____
Facsimile number _____
Staff_____
Status _____ Date _____
Note _____
Seating
Staff_____
Status _____ Date _____
Note _____
Program/menu card text
Staff_____
Status _____ Date _____
Note _____
Transportation
Staff_____
Status _____ Date _____
Note _____
Music
Staff_____
Status _____ Date _____
Note _____

Parking
Valet
Self-parking accommodation
Staff_____
Status _____ Date _____
Note _____
Staff coordination
Coordinator_____
Status _____ Date _____
Note _____

Eight
Media Relations

T he essence of media relations is an adversarial game between an organization's spokesperson and a journalist. Both participants use special skills, strategies, nuances, and methods to achieve their goals—journalists digging for facts, media relations specialists presenting their companies or clients in the best possible light. Each party understands the other's ploys and tries to neutralize them.

Even though the media relations specialist and the reporter approach a situation with different goals in mind, their relationship need not be confrontational. In fact, the professional communicator should consider every chance to speak with a broadcast or print reporter as an opportunity to advance the company's or client's status and position in the press.

Teaching media relations techniques is difficult because there is so little science and so much art involved. Media relations require skills that may border on clairvoyance. You must be able to analyze circumstances instantly (so you can predict where a reporter's interest lies) while relying on previous experience to best handle the situation. The skills required of a media relations specialist are often learned the hard way—being burned once in the press will train you to avoid the same trap in the future.

Media relations work is important but often misunderstood. It is a high-stakes, high-pressure, high-visibility communications role with little sympathy for error. The impact of a media relations expert's effort is immediate. A single news report can make or break a company's reputation and image. Media relations constitute a fast-paced area of responsibility, offering virtually instant dissemination of your company's or client's message.

Even though this chapter describes how to create, maintain, and perpetuate a successful media relations program, it cannot give you insight or intuitive judgment. Those intangible qualities must be developed by experience and honed by practice. If you observe a media relations specialist in action, however, several common characteristics surface. The most successful media relations people are calm, confident, and cooperative.

RESPONSIBILITIES AND FUNCTIONS

In a business organization, a media relations specialist receives and resolves press inquiries. He or she functions as liaison between the media and the client or company. The designated individual becomes the client's or company's spokesperson, responsible for disseminating accurate information and maintaining the client's or company's public reputation and image.

Though media queries vary, the responsibilities of a media relations expert remain constant. When the news media contact or report on a company, media relations professionals must be prepared to provide accurate information in a timely fashion and in a manner designed to protect the client's or company's image and integrity. Information provided must be consistent with established company policies. The goal is to ensure that the company or client is fairly represented in the press.

Media relations professionals perform several functions; they:

- Become the first-line contact with the media.
- Serve as spokesperson for a company or client.
- Develop communications strategies.
- Assist as a coach for interviews.
- Ensure that the company is represented accurately and positively.
- Verify that reporters talk to the best source of information and that the facts they provide are accurate and germane.
- Gather pertinent information.
- Anticipate questions and determine the best way to answer them.
- Help to develop key points the company or client wants to convey.

As a media relations professional, you may want to codify your company's or client's media response procedures. Encourage your client or company to adhere to a few simple tenets. For instance, counsel employees to contact you as soon as a reporter contacts them directly. You need to know about all media inquiries because it is your responsibility to ensure that information released to the press about your company or client is consistent and accurate. Your direct involvement is needed because you may have spoken with the reporter about the same or related topics in the past or you may have established a professional relationship with a particular reporter.

You can guide a reporter to the most informed and best qualified source of information within the organization. Most likely, the reporter will want to speak with someone who is highest ranking, immediately responsible, or most knowledgeable about a certain subject.

PREPARING YOURSELF FOR MEDIA INQUIRIES

Virtually any activity will prompt a media call:

- Good news.
- Bad news.
- Strife.
- Rumors.
- Famous or infamous individuals on staff or associated with your company or client.
- Acquisitions.
- Dispositions.
- Disasters or emergencies.
- Product introductions.
- Product recalls.
- Industry trends.

When developing responses for the media or preparing for an interview, you should lead with the most important message or news. Describe the beneficial effects of your company's or client's actions on the public interest, the economy, the environment, or other pertinent subjects without resorting to technical jargon.

Turn negative questions into positive responses. Use positive wording, especially in emergency or disaster situations. For example:

> Question: "What information do you have on the hijacking of Flight 13?"
>
> Answer: "No one has been injured aboard Flight 13, which is enroute to [an unscheduled destination]."

Do not respond to unofficial statistics or figures, but avoid saying "No comment." If you cannot supply information, explain why. Single word answers may not be best. In print, your client may be portrayed as uncooperative and sullen, and on a broadcast, one-word answers may be inserted after questions for which they were not given.

Always tell the truth and avoid injecting your personal opinions.

Avoid stonewalling an issue. "I don't know" is an acceptable answer—used sparingly. If you do not know, promise to research the topic and provide information as soon as possible after the initial interview. Be sure to fulfill your promise.

Avoid speaking off the record. Reporters dislike that condition and immediately suspect you of withholding facts or trying to manipulate the story. Press conferences require extra media relations protocol and it is much more complicated to go off the record. At a press conference, all reporters present, not just the questioner, must agree to honor your request.

Do not say anything to a reporter you don't want to read in print or see on screen. The experience of one West Coast media relations professional illustrates this clearly.

A young reporter from a small Connecticut community newspaper called the West Coast company to verify a rumor that the company was about to purchase a landmark building in a particular Connecticut town. Following company procedure, the media relations person said, "It's the XYZ Corporation's policy not to comment on rumors." The reporter asked two more questions: was it true that XYZ owned other property in Connecticut and how much were XYZ's revenues last year? The media relations specialist verified property holdings in the state and, representing a publicly held company, provided the revenue figure. He then asked, "Is there any more information I can provide?" and the reporter said no. The media relations person asked if the interview was over and was told that it was. The company spokesperson then casually said, "I'm curious for my own information. Where is your town located in Connecticut? I've never heard of it." The reporter named the two cities on either side of his town, the media relations specialist said thanks, and they both hung up.

Two days later, the vice president of XYZ's Connecticut office irately called his counterpart on the West Coast, insisting that the media relations person had "damaged us terribly." Apparently the zealous reporter had used everything in their conversation. The offending quote read, "... spokesperson for the XYZ Corporation would neither confirm nor deny the report that the company was planning to purchase the landmark building, saying 'Where is this city? I've never heard of it.'" The inaccurate implication of the story was that XYZ arrogantly thought the Connecticut town insignificant.

Everybody suffered from that experience. The townspeople were insulted by the perceived haughtiness of the corporation. The local XYZ office unhappily took the brunt of that indignation. West Coast management was stung by local Connecticut displeasure and demanded an explanation from the media liaison. The response from the media relations professional was that the interview had been officially terminated before the question about the location of the town was asked—a protocol subtlety lost on the reporter.

It is always wise to anticipate issues and practice your answers. Draft simple responses to the topics you or your client expect to address. In broadcast interviews, a 30-second sound bite, which is considered a long response, equals approximately 75 words. Target sound bites at a 10th-grade education level for maximum effectiveness.

PREPARING YOUR CLIENT
TO MEET THE PRESS

As a matter of course, and certainly before any disaster or crisis response, take the time to prepare executives to face the press. This is particularly important when their scope of knowledge and credibility are critical to a particular issue. Preparation may include the following tasks:

- Writing anticipated questions for the interviewee.
- Assisting in developing responses.
- Suggesting practice sessions.
- Rehearsing executives for interviews.

- Alerting executives or clients to possible interview pitfalls.

The most common of these pitfalls are outlined in the following sections.

False Questions

The response should always correct false information in a question before completing the answer. A useful technique is to paraphrase the question during your reply.

The Loaded Preface

Try to dissect the issues. The reporter may be trying to glean a story on some other subject from your answers. For example, if a reporter says: "Your company is notorious for cutting corners during the manufacture of its products. Was this recall expected?" Your response can be organized to highlight a positive point of view: "Our manufacturing record is one of the best in the business. We issued the recall to correct potential problems that had been discovered and to assure customers that we constantly monitor and check the products we sell."

"What-if" Questions

Do not respond to speculation or hypothetical scenarios. A sample response would be, "XYZ Corporation cannot speculate on the outcome."

False Relationship of Events

If a reporter asks, for example, "The cost of gasoline at the consumer pump has risen X percent during the past three years. Why is your firm continuing to manufacture bigger model cars?" You might reply, "We respond to consumer interest. We have no control over the price of fuel."

Popular Prejudice

A reporter might ask: "Why are you donating junk food to the homeless shelter? These people need nutritious, wholesome food." A good response would be, "Our menu is actually quite nutritious. An independent nutritional analysis [by a recognized university, hospital, or research organization] showed that our hamburgers meet an adult's daily nutritional requirements as described by the U.S. Department of Health and Human Services."

Pauses

Caution the intimidated interviewee against imagining that he or she is obligated to fill any void with more response.

Grooming and Appearance

When preparing for television appearances, make grooming and appearance suggestions. Be sure that your boss or client is dressed appropriately—many executives keep fresh changes of clothes at the office. A shirt or blouse with a light color or pattern is preferable to a white shirt or blouse, but plaid is definitely out for a broadcast appearance. Discourage jangling jewelry.

Suggest cosmetic enhancements if necessary, but be aware that discussions of make-up, hair color, beard shadow, glasses versus contact lenses, or other personal physical attributes must be handled as diplomatically as possible. Always present your suggestions by describing the benefits they will yield. Preparing your client for a video appearance is closely related to preparing him or her for a still photo. The concerns about grooming and appearance described in the "Planning a Photograph" section in chapter five apply equally here.

Verbal and Nonverbal Communications

During a videotaped interview or live television broadcast, be mindful of body language. For radio and television appearances, advise your clients to keep a tone of confidence in their voices. Many businesspeople would benefit from professional voice training.

Counsel your client to utilize linguistic transitions and links such as:

> "The main thing for the public to remember ..."
>
> "Let's look at the larger issue ..."
>
> "Let me explain our procedure ..."

PREPARING FOR AN INTERVIEW

Interviews are opportunities to provide information, communicate your message, and sway audience reaction. Virtually every media relations expert agrees that the following guidelines apply equally well to preparing your client for telephone, broadcast, or print interviews:

- Prepare in advance.
- Anticipate questions.
- Gather information and background facts before the interview.
- Determine and assess the audience.

- Rehearse the main points you want to emphasize during the interview.

The sound bites utilized by broadcasters mix the message, the presentation, and the personality of the subject almost simultaneously. The audience is forced to form opinions in as few as five seconds. Media relations, public relations, and advertising professionals know that:

- Few viewers will remember the interviewee's name.
- Few viewers will remember what he or she said.
- Viewers do tend to remember his or her affiliation.
- An audience will immediately like or dislike the individual they see on screen.

For electronic interviews, ask yourself these questions:

- Will it be on broadcast television or cable?
- Will it be aired on a local station or a network?
- Will it be a talk show, interview, analysis, commentary, or reaction piece?

For print interviews, ask yourself :

- Will it be prepared for the consumer or trade press?
- Will it appear in a magazine, newspaper, or on a wire service?
- Will it be written by a free-lance journalist or staff writer? Has a publication assigned this story, or is it being prepared on speculation? Will it definitely appear in print?

- Will it be a feature story, interview, background, analysis, or reaction piece?

DURING AN INTERVIEW

An interview is not a typical chat—the rules of conversation do not apply. Approach an interview with the understanding that the reporter represents a communications vehicle through which you reach an industry, financial, or general audience.

Spokespeople and interviewees should follow these basic principles, which coincide with points raised in the "Preparing Yourself for Media Inquiries" section.

Tell the truth. It is possible to be honest without revealing proprietary information, competitive secrets, or strategic details. A lie destroys credibility and hurts your company's reputation. It can also lead to further media investigation. The public often understands that you cannot reveal certain details for competitive, safety, or other reasons.

Avoid technical terms and industry-specific jargon. Respond to questions concisely. When possible, begin your answer with a summary statement and follow it with details.

Avoid saying "No comment." If you can't answer a question, explain why.

Respond to information within your field of knowledge. If the interview questions stray from your area of expertise, tell the reporter. You can always supply information later or direct the reporter to talk to the right person. It is acceptable to say "I don't know." Do not speculate, draw conclusions to hypothetical questions, or give information unless you are positive it is meant for public dissemination.

Maintaining confidentiality does not preclude a successful interview. Interviewees often discuss business philosophy, directions, strategies, and even some financial information while maintaining discretion. Do not respond off the record. Do not say anything to a reporter that you would not want to see in a story.

Understand the reporter's job—to dig for information. There is no need to dwell on a reporter's individual style of information gathering. Aggressiveness can often be attributed to the demands of the reporter's job—gathering information from (often reluctant) sources while adhering to deadlines. If he or she asks unpleasant or difficult questions, stick to the subject at hand and remember the information you want to impart.

In some instances, you may wish to record your interview. Reporters often do this (and should ask your permission). Politely inform the reporter you want to do the same. If he or she objects, present your position as a matter of reciprocity that will ensure fairness and accuracy. If the reporter continues to object, reconsider the interview.

Any time you have prepared a client for contact with the press, it is advisable to suggest a postinterview evaluation in order to rate the result. Did your points come through? Did you overestimate or underestimate the reporter? Did you prepare sufficiently? Did you anticipate questions? Did any questions surprise you? What would you change or improve before the next interview?

HOW TO HANDLE A PRESS CALL

Media will contact you for a variety of reasons:

- To cover a crisis or disaster.
- To follow up on a press release you issued.

- To arrange a print or broadcast interview with a famous or charismatic member of your organization.

- To record a comment on business or social trends.

- To investigate information obtained from independent sources.

Ask the reporter what specific information he or she requires. How much time do you have to respond? What is the reporter's deadline? Explain that you or someone else within the organization will respond.

Respect a reporter's deadline. Respond as quickly as possible to inquiries, but don't be pressured to provide an answer just because the reporter is on deadline. It is his or her deadline—not yours. Your primary concern is to supply accurate information. However, a delayed response gives the impression that you are uncooperative or stonewalling an issue. The reporter will probably go ahead with the story even if you don't respond. Failing to respond deprives you of the chance to contribute to the story and present your client's or company's points.

Remember, you have no *obligation* to speak to the press. Part of the media relations function requires developing a judgmental sense about when and if to respond to media questions. Generally, it is beneficial to cooperate with the press, but you need not reveal secrets. You may decline to answer questions that would require revealing confidential material in response. You should be aware that although reporters will try to obtain as much information as possible, they are usually not surprised when company spokespeople decline to respond for competitive or proprietary reasons.

Many media relations people agree that the most frustrating aspect of the job is the lack of control over the final version of the story a reporter is preparing. Be sure press releases carry all necessary information. In addition to its message, every press release should include (at least) a name to contact for more information, the contact's telephone number, and the date of issue.

HOW TO HANDLE AN INACCURACY

The reporter and, in some cases, the editor or news director, should be alerted to inaccuracies in a report. A phone call or letter is sufficient notice. Your message should be firm, reasonable, and constructive. State the problem clearly, provide correct information, and suggest a remedy. If you taped your client's interview, provide a transcript. If you supplied printed information, resubmit it.

The remedy you request and the remedy you receive may undergo an alteration during discussions. It is unreasonable to expect a publication to reprint an entire story or a television or radio station to rebroadcast a segment. The print media may offer a letter-to-the-editor forum or include your information in a correction box. Broadcast organizations rarely correct stories on the air.

MEDIA RELATIONS PROFESSIONALS AGREE

Three fundamental truisms exist:

- Media relations are as important a component of an overall communication program as advertising or direct contact with customers.

- A company's relationship with the press is usually a direct result of its corporate culture. (Review the Exxon *Valdez* and Tylenol sections of chapter two for the direct result of corporate culture on media relations.)

- Participants on both sides of the reporter's notebook or microphone share at least one trait: they both need each other to complete their tasks. The media need facts and information, which media relations representatives control. Media relations representatives need the reporter's audience of readers, viewers, or listeners.

A simple form appears below that allows you to record media telephone inquiries. The form lists the reporter's name, telephone or facsimile number, and news organization, the question the reporter asked, and the action you took to answer it. The *Action* column may show that you answered the question immediately, followed up by sending print materials, referred the call to another source, or fulfilled an interview request.

Media inquiry log

Date	Caller	From	Question	Action

Nine
Office Automation

To compete in modern business environments, you must be familiar with the range of communications tasks possible in an automated office. It is essential to understand the functions hardware and software perform. Yes, you must learn how to operate the equipment. Eventually, that knowledge becomes second nature and allows you to maximize the equipment's capabilities. Of course, you or your employer will have to spend some money. Increased productivity and instant access to information more than justify the financial investment.

An automated office pairs the communicator with interactive electronic tools in his or her immediate work space. The tools help the communicator create, produce, collect, and distribute information for his or her client or company. The interactive aspect of the tools means that their service or function is available to a communicator at any time and that the communicator can operate the system with sufficient proficiency to complete the task required and obtain an immediate response.

An automated office is essential. It increases your productivity, streamlines your method of operation, keeps creation costs down, and enables you to present a professional image to your boss or client.

Think about how a business communicator can utilize an automated office. What can technology do for you? How can a business communicator manipulate or exploit the automated services to his or her benefit or the benefit of his or her client or company?

Automated office equipment is merely the tool you use to achieve your communications goals efficiently and cost-effectively. You are in command. The machines speed up the process, but they don't supply the content.

EQUIPMENT AND
AUTOMATED OFFICE NEEDS

Today, virtually anyone with a personal computer (PC) and laser printer can create stationery, brochures, magazines, posters, bulletins, and signage—everything a business needs to communicate with internal or external audiences.

Today's necessary tools and options are:

- Telephone.
- Copier.
- Typewriter.
- Facsimile machine.
- Personal computer with printer.
- PC software for word processing, desktop publishing, graphics, and financial functions such as accounting and billing.
- Modem.

- Color copier.
- Color printer.
- Color scanner.
- CD-ROM player.
- Electronic mail network.
- Voice mail.

Recently, office equipment manufacturers have begun marketing machinery offering multiple capabilities. Personal computer products that were formerly sold separately are being rolled into a single unit—much like stereo systems that contain a cassette tape player, a compact disc player, and a radio. When personal computers were first introduced, the hard disk, modem, or disk drives were purchased individually. Most PCs sold in mass-market channels today come with modems, monitors, software, and, in some cases, printers as components of a complete package. A similar trend combines phone-line products. Facsimile, answering unit (voice mail), and copier capabilities are commonly found in one unit. Some of these products plug into a PC. Eventually, voice mail features will be reduced to microchips and will be sold as part of a telephone.

AUTOMATING COMMUNICATIONS TASKS

The creation and distribution of virtually every communications product or service has been and will continue to be improved with electronic assistance.

Creating Publications and Visual Materials

Desktop publishing.   Software that manipulates words and graphics has developed into desktop publishing, a useful and necessary office tool. Desktop publishing revolutionizes the publishing and graphic design businesses because it saves money, is faster than traditional publication assembly methods, requires minimal hardware, and is compatible with desktop computers.

Even though text and graphics may be created in the desktop-publishing software programs, few of them have full word-processing and graphics capabilities. Often, work is created outside the desktop-publishing system (in word-processing, computer-aided design, or paint programs) and imported into the system. Desktop-publishing programs accept common file formats.

Major desktop publishing features are the abilities to merge and manage text and graphics and to display them in their formatted form on a computer screen. However, keep in mind that the professional look of printed materials results from experience. Desktop publishing is no substitute for a graphic designer familiar with type fonts and page layout.

Graphics. Improvements in software have allowed communicators to create finished graphics at their workplaces. Inexpensive software programs provide professional graphic artists' tools on personal computers. Many graphics programs come with extensive clip-art libraries.

Visuals. Technology has also reduced the cost of equipment capable of producing slides and overhead transparencies. Photocopy machines and laser printers produce overheads on acetate as easily as they print on paper.

Video. Desktop video provides a full range of video editing and production functions. Even though tools for video publishing have not developed as rapidly as tools for print projects, the evolutionary pattern will be the same. As hardware becomes less expensive and more readily available and operational standards emerge, desktop video will grow in popularity.

Receiving, Collecting, and Distributing Information via Technology

Audiotex.   Audiotex is a voice response application that allows users to enter and retrieve information via touch-tone telephone. Callers obtain specific information from a menu of choices. ("Press 1 for information about ...")

Increasingly, corporate clients have begun utilizing audiotex in 800/900 telephone number service applications. For example, shareholders unable to travel to the site of an annual meeting could dial a 900 number, pay the fee (which helps cover installation and operation costs), and hear the annual meeting as it is presented live. This telephone service is essentially a broadcast that allows callers to hear proceedings from remote venues. In another example, 800 numbers could allow employees to inquire, toll-free, about health benefits, the details of a new program, discounts on company merchandise, policy changes, or almost any other information an employer might want to disseminate. Obtainable from the large telecommunications carriers, 800 and 900 numbers provide nationwide, regional, or local coverage.

Data bases.   Computer data bases are of two types: CD-ROM, accessed by personal computer and CD-ROM player, and on-line services, accessed by personal computer and modem. The acronym CD-ROM stands for "compact disc—read only memory," a computer storage and distribution medium that utilizes the same compact discs used for audio recordings. When used for storage, a single compact disc can hold up to 600 million characters—roughly 300,000 book pages of information. A CD-ROM drive attached to a personal computer reads the information on the disc.

CD-ROMs carry an ever-increasing array of information. Encyclopedias, texts, periodicals, and research reports on specific topics (such as securities investments, business, politics, social sciences, market share of new products, mergers, acquisitions, and financial analyses) are available on disc. Depending on the disc provided, CD-ROMs either contain the document's full text or an abstract. In the latter case, the data base would tell you where to look up the actual information in full.

On-line data base services deliver information on a variety of topics to a PC through a modem. A user pays a fixed rate to get into the data base and is then charged for the amount of time used, including printing time. Charges for individual data bases vary. However, the amount of information they carry, the speed with which information can be found, and the frequency with which they are updated make them attractive.

To access a data base, a user's modem contacts and connects to the desired service. Using previously defined software parameters, the user instructs then the data base to find specific information. For example, you could request your company's or client's stock price information from a financial services data base. In addition, you could also tell the data base to send news stories about your company or client to specific destinations such as business associates (assuming the addressees have the capability to receive) or to a printer. The only human actions required are a few key strokes.

Distributing this information electronically is also possible. Since it already resides in your computer, you can merely format it and electronically mail it to anyone in the organization. The material will remain in the receiver's electronic mailbox until it is read, printed, or otherwise utilized. This method of information distribution is well suited for a company that is spread out in several satellite locations.

In general, on-line services or data bases are best used to gather detailed information from many sources. They are helpful when gathering research for major presentations, executive speeches, or for custom-tailored tasks such as determining how many times a competitor is mentioned in the consumer or trade press.

On-line services and data bases are compilation services. Think of them as one-stop shopping stores. You need only go to one place to find information, but you pay a premium price for the convenience.

Electronic mail (e-mail).   Electronic mail is a computer-based system, accessed by personal computer with network software, which allows individuals to prepare, read, route, and print information. A good comparison is the arrangement by which one retrieves or sends correspondence from a post office box. Boxes are private, so you must check them to find out when mail arrives. Another similarity is that most systems allow you to prepare your mail "off-line," that is while you are not connected to an electronic mail network. You then connect and mail your messages (go to the post office and mail the letters).

Be careful not to put sensitive information on an e-mail system. Like cellular telephones, some e-mail systems are not secure.

Facsimile (fax).   This is the standard technology for transmitting printed images using telephone connections and a facsimile machine.

"Fax on demand" combines a voice mail system with a facsimile machine for unattended operation. Callers can request information from prerecorded voice menus, hang up, then wait for the information to arrive via their fax machine.

Satellite transmissions and teleconferences. Satellite uplink and downlink to television monitors at predetermined receiving sites provides access to electronic communications services, which allow the exchange of live video and audio images simultaneously between two or more locations.

Video and audio teleconferencing require a business communicator to think like a broadcasting producer and director. Important issues are camera and microphone placement, seating arrangements, lighting, make-up for participants, wardrobe, visual support materials, and live editing.

Video news releases. Visual press releases are provided to broadcast or cablecast sources. Delivery is possible on video cassette or via satellite transmission. The advantage of a video news release is the visual impact that helps tell your story.

Videotex. Videotex is two-way, interactive television, which is fed into home or office television receivers (modified with ancillary hardware) via telephone, cable television, or fiber optic lines. Users can push a few buttons and read a newspaper, order merchandise from catalogs, book travel reservations, perform banking functions, check the weather, peruse entertainment listings, or play games on a television screen at home or in an office.

Voice mail. Voice mail, accessed by touch-tone telephone, works similarly to e-mail. However, it is better suited to shorter messages and smaller amounts of information. There are two big differences between voice mail and electronic mail. While routing or forwarding e-mail messages between systems is possible, it is not common practice to route voice mail messages between systems. The other difference is the level of detail that the medium supports. If users want to save a voice mail message, they must write down the information.

Electronic distribution services are available to serve an external audience. By supplying a service provider with the company's or client's stationery and transmitting the list of receivers' names and addresses, press releases, reports, or other pieces of information can be sent electronically. If addressees have a compatible electronic mailbox, they can receive transmissions instantly; if they do not, information is automatically printed on laser printers, folded, stuffed into an envelope, and sent. The following day, all addressees have the material on their desks. The speed of such a procedure allows your client or company to contact potential customers, contacts, or business prospects who may not have read the press release from the wire services or in print.

Wire services.   Wire services distribute your press release via telephone, personal computer with modem, data base, vendor-supplied printer, or subscription to their subscribers, including print and broadcast outlets around the country. Media must subscribe to the service before they receive your release.

There are general-news wire services, special-interest wire services, and geographically specific wire services. They may be found in city phone books, through public relations directories, in *Editor & Publisher*, *PR Journal*, and other media publications. You may send information to them by mail, telephone, or electronically. Some services charge you a fee—usually by the word—to put material on their wire.

ACQUIRING EQUIPMENT

Consider the acquisition of office equipment one of the costs of doing business. The required investment in time and money can, and should, be made incrementally. Let the volume of work you produce dictate the equipment you need, when to acquire the equipment, and how much time you can dedicate to learning its capabilities.

Before Shopping for Equipment

Find out what office machines your clients use. For example, most business communicators and creative services providers use Macintosh computers. Because it is often necessary to exchange work in progress, you may save money if you can deliver documents in a format supported by your graphic designer, typesetter, or printer.

While Shopping for Equipment

Do not immediately purchase all the electronic toys you want. Get equipment on loan from a vendor, try it out in a retail store, or borrow friends' equipment. This way, you can determine the kind of equipment and the features you need.

Choose widely used software. Do not buy software that offers more features than you will use. There is no use paying for unnecessary capabilities.

Economize on your personal computer but not on your printer. Clients will be looking at your product, not at your hardware.

Ten

Preparing for a Corporate Communications Career

There is a myth that corporate communicators make poor executives. Because so many professional communicators have journalism backgrounds, the odd logic goes, they are more comfortable as conduits than as leaders. This conclusion gives business-trained colleagues in other departments the erroneous idea that communicators shun or ignore business responsibilities. In fact, organization and supervision are two skills that corporate communicators must employ in order to blend communications programs with business goals.

The previous chapters have emphasized ways in which business communications careers demand a combination of creativity and technical knowledge. Corporate communicators must be able to plan, produce, and deliver a wide range of materials and events. Their responsibilities include determining the most effective and economical medium or media to employ in producing print materials such as reports, magazines, brochures, advertisements, rosters, manuals, speech reprints, programs, and invitations.

The communications specialist must also secure the best available service provider the budget will allow for producing visual materials such as photographs, artwork, graphics, videos, and multi-image presentations. For special events including luncheons, dinners, award programs, product introductions, shareholders' meetings, fund-raisers, and tours, the corporate communicator must establish the purpose and goal of the event, then plan it as if he or she were a guest.

The communications specialist must also be familiar with many technical advances in the business world. These include the current generation of electronic office equipment: PCs, modems, graphic software, and desktop-publishing software. Communicators utilize modems and diskettes as efficient and cost-effective media for sending and receiving materials.

Similarly, communication experts must be familiar with electronic distribution channels such as PR Newswire, BusinessWire, and similar services, which for a fee, distribute your message to target audiences.

Data base retrieval, the capability of obtaining information from several sources in one electronic repository, is another technical field of increasing importance to the communications person. Newspapers and magazines, university research materials, business and professional histories, and an ever-growing slate of information now reside on data bases.

Interactive media are also valuable new tools for business communications. These include videotex, two-way or interactive television; and audiotex, two-way or interactive aural services. These media allow the user to tell the television or telephone to provide only the specific information he or she orders from a menu of choices.

It is also the responsibility of the corporate communicator to discover and exploit ancillary uses for personal computers. Their use for illustrative purposes at meetings or press conferences and as media of communications are only a few examples of their potential.

YOUR EFFECTIVENESS

Your effectiveness as a corporate communications professional can be maximized by keeping some simple points in mind. In a corporate environment, these four elements are essential for successful communications programs:

(1) Creativity and talent.

(2) Money.

(3) Staff. The help of people with whom you work well and who possess the information, capabilities, and skills to complete communications tasks should not be underestimated. Support staff supply vital assistance.

(4) Management support.

Even if you possess these four essential factors, you must be prepared to deal with the realities of business life. While working on any communication project, expect some negative input.

Such input may come in the form of management scrutiny. Some managers who may be unfamiliar with the creative process or the communications function, will dissect or reject your ideas.

You will always be asked about expenses, costs, and fees when you pitch ideas or suggest courses of action. Undoubtedly, you will come up against instructions or admonitions from higher-ups asking you to stretch your resources. Be prudent about spending money. Management does not want to provide carte blanche, but it does want the most outstanding product possible.

You will also certainly face questions about personnel requirements. You will be asked, "Does it really take so many people to create this?" "Why do you have to pay a consultant?" "Why do you have to go to outside vendors?" Have answers ready.

At some companies, the corporate communications department is regarded as a necessary evil. Some executives claim the communications function costs huge sums of money to maintain and brings nothing to the bottom line. That old-fashioned view is being dispelled, however, as businesspeople become more comfortable with the increasing array of affordable and easy-to-use media. In addition, many corporations have reassessed their communications programs and now realize their proven value.

YOUR USEFULNESS

Your usefulness in business communications can be maximized through creativity and talent. These are your most important resources.

In addition, you should develop and demonstrate a working expertise in some special skill. Augment the requirements that appear in your job description. The most common areas of adjunct expertise are:

- Editorial.

- Print production.
- Film.
- Video.
- Multi-image production.
- Event planning.
- Electronic communication/office automation.
- Telecommunications (satellite transmissions, tele-conferencing, putting together news conferences).

Management support is essential. No project you want to produce will proceed without management endorsement. To attract management or client support, describe the benefit your program will deliver to the company or client.

After management support is obtained, projects begin. Project approval entails the allocation of funds. It is safe to assume that there has never been a situation in which a communications person, a public relations professional, or an event planner had too much cash for a project. The amount of money and the scope of resources your boss or client dedicates to a project is tied to the client's or organization's perception of the communications function.

If management or the client sees your service as a benefit, project money comes your way. If you can sell your project idea or proposal to a finance-oriented executive or a senior executive concerned with bottom-line expenses, your proposal is probably good and stands a strong chance of success in the market.

It is incumbent on the creative personality functioning within an organization to be aware of the business concerns and business realities of his or her company or client. Conversely, it would be helpful if the business personalities—people who are geared to empirical evidence—showed reciprocity and extended creative latitude to the communications staff.

Finally, demonstrate flexibility—be willing to absorb new information, new techniques, new methods of accomplishing tasks. The increasing pervasiveness of electronics and technology in communications makes this tenet obvious. Today's communications jobs require different skills and training than they did three years ago. In three more years, the skills required could emphasize technological background more strongly than practical experience. Resourcefulness and flexibility are traits you will need to develop and demonstrate if they do not already come to you naturally. Seeking new methods of completing projects, especially if they result in cost savings, shows management you are interested in and informed about new developments within your industry.

DO YOU AND YOUR COMPANY MATCH?

You must determine if you and your company have a future together. When you choose an employer, you choose a way of life. You have three choices of action if you discover that your style conflicts with your company's or client's established culture.

First, you can change the culture to suit you. This is tough to accomplish unless you enter an organization at a sufficiently high level of management to actually and credibly institute change. For entry-level employees and middle managers, the possibility of altering a company's culture is unlikely but not impossible. The same management patronage described in the previous section is essential to transform, bend, or modify existing corporate culture.

Second, you can adapt as well as possible for as long as you can. Like a staring contest, this course becomes nothing more than a waiting game to see which party flinches first. Frustration, anxiety, and stress develop on both sides.

Third, and most obvious, you can change companies.

This concern of fitting comfortably within an organization surfaces often during discussions with colleagues. In one story, a communications specialist from a small publishing house in Connecticut was offered a higher-level position at an entertainment firm in California. Of course, she accepted immediately. She arrived in Southern California eager and excited. Her responsibilities required her to produce a quarterly employee magazine, help prepare a portion of the annual report, and assist her boss with a quarterly report made available to the press—not a heavy work load.

During the first four months, all went well. Her co-workers were pleasant and friendly, the fringe benefits (such as the opportunity to see the company's motion pictures free of charge and the deep discounts available on recordings and books) were agreeable and the money was good. Soon thereafter, however, she realized her methodical work pattern did not correspond with the company's style. Even though the volume of her responsibilities did not increase, she found the pace of her new environment overwhelming. She was not used to short deadlines and quick project completion cycles. She was unused to multiple layers of scrutiny. She was often required to defend her level of technical knowledge and to justify administrative and artistic decisions. She disliked working in a team atmosphere, which she considered invasive. She interpreted suggestions as criticisms. New assignments translated into evenings and weekends at the office. All these factors added up to an unacceptable work setting.

The traditional sources of remedy she had used to solve problems in Connecticut—talking to peers, receiving occasional nods of approval from her boss, or in extreme cases, seeking counsel from the personnel department—did not offer satisfaction. Ultimately, she left the entertainment company and settled into the communications department of a bank. She found the controlled office atmosphere and the established patterns of authority pleasing. Her new contentment led to increased productivity and the ability to add comfortably to the scope of her responsibilities.

There are many examples of talented, dedicated, hard-working employees who cannot perform at peak levels because they find themselves in the wrong company culture. That discovery can lead to discontent, which opens the door to stress-related anxieties. The quality and quantity of work usually suffer, as do both the employee's and employer's attitudes. When those same people move to a company where they perceive a better cultural fit, they perform optimally.

COMPETITION

Competition for corporate communications jobs is intense. To present yourself more favorably than a competitor, accumulate as many credentials as possible. Obtain as much formal education as you can. Augment your formal education with classes of specific interest or turn a hobby or personal avocation into an information resource. Almost any source of endeavor can provide information useful to the communications function. In the minds of potential employers or clients, outside information combined with a formal education and professional experience places you ahead of competitors.

Be as informed as possible. Trade-group meetings and periodicals are useful. Call the International Association of Business Communicators at (415) 433-3400, for local chapter information and to obtain a subscription to its publication, *Communications World.*

COMMUNICATIONS PHILOSOPHY

Each project or client is unique and must be assessed as such. Do not think of communications tasks as rote performances. No two jobs are the same. Each is an independent entity requiring a fresh approach. Your technique and skill may be reapplied, but the content of each assignment will be different.

Regardless of the information in question, one communications tenet will hold true: the message is valueless unless it is received *and* understood. Effective communication requires both receipt and comprehension by your audience. You can send a message electronically, aurally, or physically on paper, but if no one receives it, it has gone nowhere. By the same token, you can send information or messages effectively and attractively, but if your audience does not or cannot understand it, your company's or client's time and money have been wasted.

You must always ask yourself:

- Who is the audience?
- What do you want them to know?
- What reaction do you want from your audience?
- How will you send your information or message? (What medium or which combination of media would be most effective?)

- How will the audience receive the information? (Will your message be presented in a favorable or adversarial environment?)
- What will it take to reach your target audience (how much time and money)?
- What will be the effect of individual corporate communications projects on the clients, products, or services you represent and the corporate culture?
- Most importantly, will your boss or client be well served?

Corporate communications is undoubtedly the most dynamic field to be aspiring to or practicing in today's business environment. The logical interdependence of communications and emerging technologies requires the effective practitioner's skills to be state of the art and cutting edge. The insistence upon creativity and resourcefulness ensures that the successful practitioner will be continuously challenged and tested. Make no mistake—corporate communications is an exacting and demanding profession. Consequently, it is also one of the most satisfying.

Eleven

The Origins of Corporate Communications

T he need for communications departments in modern corporations was a direct result of basic changes in the nature of American business, which began in the 1920s. The country had been rapidly industrializing since the end of the Civil War. By the end of the 19th century, companies typically remained small, regionally based concerns. During the 1920s, however, business and industry took on a distinctly modern appearance and began to resemble the corporate structure we know today. In the 1920s, sociologist Robert Lynd[1] identified several basic factors changing American business:

---

[1]Robert S. Lynd and Helen Merrell Lynd, *Middletown: A Study in Contemporary American Culture* (New York: Brace & Company, 1929).

- Large factories were employing between 1,000 and 2,000 workers, compared to approximately 200 workers a generation before.

- Employers no longer knew their employees.

- Industrial hierarchies of technically trained managers were multiplying.

- Larger, less personal chain stores supplanted independent retailers.

- New forms of consumer credit accelerated economic activity. Buying houses, cars, and appliances was easier.

- The country was becoming more urban and consumers more sophisticated.

The changes in American industry and commerce gave rise to a mass commercial culture. New and better forms of media, principally radio, roadside billboards, and broad-circulation magazines, allowed companies to create a uniform public image on a regional or even national basis. For the first time, corporations were able to integrate public relations with advertising programs using improved graphics in magazines and exciting sound effects on radio. The results were distributed or broadcast over a company's entire marketing area. By the 1920s, a seller's market could encompass the entire nation.

CHANGING TIMES

The gigantic interdependent corporate economy created during the 1920s forced businesspeople to discard established beliefs and rely on modern management strategies. Traditional 19th-century values such as self-reliance, individualism, and independence became outmoded. Business executives and experts all over America began telling their employees to get with the new rules of the game: cooperate, depend on others, play as a team member.

The need for greater cooperation signaled the need for a fully integrated system of corporate communication—a system that provided communication between corporation and shareholder; manufacturer, retailer, and consumer; employer and employee.

Throughout the decade of the 1920s, corporate communications adopted a modern character, particularly among companies whose products and services were based on the emerging technology of the period. All of a sudden, companies producing automobiles, appliances, electricity, and petroleum wanted their advertisements and public relations programs to employ the brightest graphics, the most up-to-date styles, and the latest psychological techniques.

Ad creators of the 1920s were part of the new business order—the missionaries of modernity. Constantly and unabashedly, they championed the new against the old, the fresh against the traditional. Advertising and corporate image building tended to be contemporary in tone, ambitious in scope, and extravagant in cost.

THE DEPRESSION

The first years of the 1930s changed corporate spending patterns. The Depression affected the entire business hierarchy from capitalist to shareholder, from producer to consumer. While the public had been generally supportive of business during the 1920s, it condemned business during the following decade.

The causes of the Depression were pinned squarely on corporate business practices of the 1920s: too much credit, too much ambitious expansion, and too much reliance on continued prosperity. The result was a crisis in prestige for business.

Corporate communications during the period reflected business's concern about its poor standing with the public. Programs became more conservative, more serious, more responsible, more austere, and better planned. They were calculated to alter opinion rather than to sell a product or create an attractive image. During this period, corporate communications were utilized to improve a negative image.

Nevertheless, intercompany corporate communications during the 1930s were frequently inadequate. Companies would make do with a mere memo stuffed into the office mailbox or a general notice tacked to a communal bulletin board. Policies for employees were handled on a department-by-department basis and not standardized throughout the company. People were hired and fired according to a manager's personal set of rules. Vacation leave was granted or retirement benefits determined on the whim of an individual.

An example of early corporate communication is this bulletin sent out by a newspaper company in 1932:

June 2, 1932

TO ALL EMPLOYEES:

The world wide bad economic situation, long continued, makes it a necessity for the company to reduce as far as practical its operating expenses if we are to continue to maintain the institution on a sound basis.

We have, through the unusual loyalty of the employees so affected up to this time, been able to make substantial reductions by shortening hours of the day or days of the week, and through effecting other economies, that we were not compelled a long time ago, as were most employers everywhere, (including practically all the newspaper establishments in the country) to reduce our force or make a flat reduction in compensation,—a matter of no small satisfaction to us all.

After giving this subject most careful consideration, the management decided to make a flat 10% reduction of the compensation of all employees who have not heretofore had their compensation reduced through the "staggering" of employment. This reduction, in order to make it absolutely equitable, will also apply to part-time employees, those paid on a bonus, commission, space or other basis,—the intention being that the several months of reduction made necessary by varying conditions shall apply without the slightest discrimination to all from the top to the bottom. The change ordered will be effective on payrolls starting on and after June 3, 1932, and until revoked.

While we all regret the necessity of this action, it is proper to consider that the purchasing power of the compensation received after the 10% reduction will be much greater than it was during the prosperous years up to the time of the stock panic in 1929, followed by the bad business conditions which have been becoming generally worse since that time.

I hope and believe that every member of the [company] family will appreciate the necessity for the reduction now made, and will continue in the future as in the past to put into his or her work all the intelligence, energy, good-will and loyalty that the situation demands.

[Signed]

President and General Manager

Pay attention to the language of this bulletin. Note how the message is worded and presented. It is verbose, yet forceful. The fact that take-home pay was to be reduced 10 percent was not addressed until the third paragraph. Significantly, the highest ranking officer in the company signed it. That level of authority could not be questioned.

The Depression had other effects on corporate communication. Apart from the necessity of creating better communications to improve business's reputation among employees and the public, certain New Deal legislation actually mandated better communication practices. The Securities Act of 1933 required better accounting by stock-issuing corporations, and the Securities and Exchange Act of 1934 created the Securities and Exchange Commission (SEC) to regulate trading practices and to force full disclosure of information. Companies were required to supply to shareholders and the federal government more complete information about publicly traded securities and about their financial condition. The result was a new "reporting" role for corporations.

CORPORATE COMMUNICATIONS THRIVE

As the economy recovered from the economic crisis, employees demanded and received better treatment from employers. Companies established uniform personnel policies and impressive lists of employee benefits. With these improvements, companies devised better, more professional ways of communicating with employees.

By the late 1930s, many companies produced booklets to describe employee status and benefits that looked much like the slick, professional publications we see today. This was a direct result of the growing corporate structure of the time.

Companies emerged from the period with a host of departments designed to manage the new, complex structure of American corporations. Corporate communications departments became an essential means of managing the relationship with employees, the public, and shareholders. A defined corporate image and corporate culture could be communicated as an integrated package.

WARTIME

In the 1940s, corporate communications went to war. The workplace itself became a medium of communication. Offices and factories were festooned with inspirational as well as precautionary messages for workers. Posters warned that loose lips sunk ships. Billboards extolled the benefits of a strong American work force supplying vital materials to combat troops. Pay envelopes contained reminders to buy war bonds. Rallies at manufacturing sites urged workers to greater production goals. Simple catch-phrases and vivid graphics conveyed the era's life-or-death urgency.

During the war years, women entered the work force to fill jobs left vacant by conscription and enlistments. These women became the focal point of many pieces of visual communication. In addition to print media, women were seen frequently in the burgeoning number of training films hastily created to spur the flow of production.

After the war, corporate communications evolved into an essential aspect of a business agenda. Reflecting the commercial expansion of the late 1940s and 1950s, the applications of business communications grew more quickly and the effects reached a wider audience than at any other time in history.

DEVELOPING WORLDWIDE MARKETS

While American businesses established themselves as multinational enterprises after World War II, their communications needs expanded exponentially. Worldwide markets for American products and services required an explanation of American business habits and procedures to multicultural work forces. Establishing manufacturing plants, constructing hotels, or opening offices in remote locations across the globe required a variety of corporate communications media. Print and visual proposals had to be created to garner local permission to construct buildings. Construction details and equipment installation instructions had to be distributed to contractors. The buildings needed signage. Employees had to be trained with company-created books and films. The challenges for professional business communicators were to ensure the integrity of the information after translation and to respect local culture.

FIGHTING NEGATIVE PERCEPTIONS

The 1960s, of course, are widely recognized as years of upheaval. The social and political divisiveness that developed in American society was fueled largely by the split reactions to the war in Viet Nam. Corporations, whether war-related materials suppliers or not, were vilified and suffered their lowest popular image in 30 years.

Business's tarnished reputation presented a dilemma to communications professionals. College campuses, strongholds of antiwar and antiwar/antibusiness sentiment, were also the traditional recruiting turf for new generations of management. How did corporate America attract potential employees while fighting negative public perception? There is no single answer. Some companies chose to address the problem directly. Attempts to sway popular thinking in favor of business were admirable but futile considering the change in social attitudes. The majority of corporations dismissed the problem as insignificant. Shareholders continued to invest, contracts were awarded, and employees preferred paychecks to pink slips. Business was good. Many companies saw no reason to initiate probusiness communications campaigns.

Looking back, both reactions had merit. Even though active communication was (and continues to be) the noblest practice for addressing problems, it is also the most resource-consuming. In addition, the hardliners were ultimately proven correct in regard to the cyclical quality of social displeasure. As we know, public opinion changed when the war ended and college students of the 1960s entered the job market.

THE RISE OF SOCIAL RESPONSIBILITY

The idealism of the 1960s was not completely smothered by corporate life. The tenets of the Aquarian Age manifested themselves in an era of socially responsible communications that surfaced in the 1970s. One of the most pronounced and long-lasting messages of that time was the rise in ecological concerns. Oil companies, chemical manufacturers, mine operators, real estate developers, and other industries with sensitive operations became responsive to public reaction. Business communicators seamlessly and inventively bridged chasms between consumption and preservation. Defoliant manufacturers decided to protect wetlands, strip miners began reforestation programs, and oil pipelines were raised off the ground so caribou herds could roam unimpeded.

Another phenomenon of the 1970s was the rise of alternative corporate cultures. Work environments developed that prized creativity, innovation, and the free flow of ideas. Computer software companies and the entertainment industry in particular gained reputations as havens for engineers and artists who eschewed traditional corporate style. Specifically, campuslike venues, intellectual freedom, and unstructured managerial organization were (and continue to be) cited in high-tech and entertainment company recruitment materials.

YEARS OF PROSPERITY

The business-friendly 1980s bred communications that glorified the power, prestige, and potential of corporate America. Business communicators had money, supportive management, and audiences eager to devour information. Investment offers and business proposals in slick packages kept in-house communications staffs and business communications consultants busy for many years.

Two significant fields of communication matured during the 1980s. The first was the rise of video as an accepted business medium. The second was the increasing importance of independent communications consultants, most notably in the area of employee health care. Many companies, reacting to or anticipating employee interest in specific topics but unable to dedicate in-house staff, hired independent communications consultants to provide turnkey packages. These specialized consultants were (and are) capable of preparing fliers, brochures, pay envelope stuffers, posters, employee magazine articles, telephone-based audio information services, videos, and an array of promotional merchandise for employee audiences. The unique knowledge of these consultants allowed employers to fulfill efficiently their information obligations while effectively answering employees' fundamental questions.

HARSH MESSAGES FOR HARSH TIMES

So far, the sour business climate of the 1990s has forced corporate communicators into the role of apologists. Many gentle euphemisms have been invented to describe downturns in business, employee layoffs, cutbacks in services, and other manifestations of recession. Executive speeches, annual reports, letters to shareholders, and employee relations bulletins have been carefully crafted to minimize unpleasant news without sacrificing the intent of the message.

THE POWER OF CORPORATE COMMUNICATIONS

These historic developments illustrate the business world's growing respect for the power to control action and create opinion. But the novelty of company-controlled information faded as the number and size of corporate employers grew in post–World War II America.

As individual companies' work forces grew, so did the necessity to introduce, broadcast, implement, and update information. The corporate communications specialist was born. The development of professional corporate communicators, the refinement of their duties, the prestige of the corporate communications function, and the steadily increasing power of corporate communicators sprang from the requirements of two sources—the group that needed to impart information and the group that needed to receive it. Today, these two entities constitute a corporate communicator's raison d'être.

The group that needs to impart information—an organization or client—acts as patron. That entity provides the corporate communicator with money, personnel, equipment, and the venue to create, maintain, and preserve an internal and external company image. The audiences for which the image is created represent the balance of a corporate communicator's professional concern. Employee audiences require and deserve information about every aspect of their professional lives. The press demands explanations of actions and motives. By law, stockholders must receive regular reports about the state of the company's or client's business. Community leaders, governmental regulators, and elected representatives must be swayed to a specific point of view.

Every audience needs information, and every individual within those audiences wants it. The professional corporate communicator is the instrument to provide that information.

Appendix

Graphic design cost estimate sheet

Date _____

Client _____

Project title_____

Project description/design services required _____

_____

_____

_____

_____

Itemized expenses

Design time _____hours @ $_____ per hour	$_____
Production time _____hours @ $_____ per hour	$_____
Illustration/photography fees	$_____
Material and supplies	$_____
Photographic prints	$_____
Printing	$_____
Typesetting	$_____
Photostats	$_____
Messengers	$_____
Shipping	$_____
Other (specify)	$_____
TOTAL	$_____
Sales tax	$_____
GRAND TOTAL	$_____

Printing estimate and quote sheet

___Quote   Date_____

___Estimate   Purchase order number _____

Job description _____

_____

_____

_____

_____

Printing specifications

Size_____

Pages _____

Paper stock _____

Quantity_____   No overs or unders _____

Number of colors_____

Inks_____

Bleeds _____

Screen tints _____

Halftones_____

Duotones_____

Color separations_____

Folding _____

Scoring_____

Bindery _____

Foil _____

Embossing_____

Die cuts _____

Packing _____

Delivery instructions_____

_____

Notes _____

_____

_____

_____

Client contact _____

Photography release form

I hereby agree that all photographs, negatives, prints, paintings, drawings, sketches, reproductions, and likenesses of any kind made of me or submitted by me to The XYZ Company are and shall remain the property of XYZ, its successors and assigns. I give my irrevocable consent that said works, or any part thereof, may be published, displayed, reproduced, and circulated in any form by XYZ or anyone else authorized by XYZ, with or without my name, for commercial purposes or otherwise, including advertisements in any media and with or without any testimonial copy or other form of advertising or display. I am over 18 years of age.

Date _____

Name _____
(Please print)
Signature _____

Name of minor _____
The above-named is a minor, and as parent or guardian of said minor, I agree to the terms of this release.
Date _____
Signature _____

Video budget planning sheet

Date _____

Project title _____

Producer _____

Address _____

Telephone _____

Facsimile _____

Project deadline date _____

Budget guideline

	Rate	Day/hour	Total
Producer	___.___ ×	_____	___.___
Director	___.___ ×	_____	___.___
Storyboard artist	___.___ ×	_____	___.___
Camera operator	___.___ ×	_____	___.___
Videotape	___.___ ×	_____	___.___
Sound mixer	___.___ ×	_____	___.___
Boom operator	___.___ ×	_____	___.___
Radio microphones	___.___ ×	_____	___.___
Lighting technician	___.___ ×	_____	___.___
Talent/actor(s)	___.___ ×	_____	___.___
	___.___ ×	_____	___.___
	___.___ ×	_____	___.___
	___.___ ×	_____	___.___
Extras	___.___ ×	_____	___.___
Makeup/hair artist	___.___ ×	_____	___.___
Catering	___.___ ×	_____	___.___
Props	___.___ ×	_____	___.___
Special camera operator	___.___ ×	_____	___.___
Insurance	___.___ ×	_____	___.___
Scouting costs	___.___ ×	_____	___.___
Travel and living	___.___ ×	_____	___.___

Vehicle rentals   _____.___ × _____   _____.___
Stage rental   _____.___ × _____   _____.___
Location rental   _____.___ × _____   _____.___
Permits   _____.___ × _____   _____.___
Doctor/nurse   _____.___ × _____   _____.___
Police/guards   _____.___ × _____   _____.___
Firefighters   _____.___ × _____   _____.___
Special equipment   _____.___ × _____   _____.___
  Steadicam   _____.___ × _____   _____.___
  Wind machine   _____.___ × _____   _____.___
  TelePromptR unit   _____.___ × _____   _____.___
  Underwater gear   _____.___ × _____   _____.___
  Walkie-talkies   _____.___ × _____   _____.___
  Bullhorn   _____.___ × _____   _____.___
  Batteries/power   _____.___ × _____   _____.___
Postproduction   _____.___ × _____   _____.___
On-line edit bay   _____.___ × _____   _____.___
Time code copies   _____.___ × _____   _____.___
Videotape editor   _____.___ × _____   _____.___
Visual effects   _____.___ × _____   _____.___
Music   _____.___ × _____   _____.___
Composer   _____.___ × _____   _____.___
Studio time   _____.___ × _____   _____.___
Musicians/singers   _____.___ × _____   _____.___
Copyrights   _____.___ × _____   _____.___

   TOTAL   _____.___
   Taxes   _____.___
    GRAND TOTAL   _____.___

Video client requirement and profile form

Date _____

Prepared by _____

Project title _____

Client/company _____

Contact/department_____

Client address_____

_____

Telephone _____

Program topic_____

Purpose _____

_____

Target audience _____

_____

Desired reaction of audience after viewing program _____

_____

_____

_____

Final distribution and viewing environment _____

_____

_____

_____

Projected production schedule _____

_____

Projected production budget_____

_____

Special production considerations _____

_____

Crew _____

_____

_____

_____

Locations_____

_____

_____

Talent _____

_____

_____

_____

_____

Equipment_____

_____

Effects_____

_____

_____

Other _____

_____

_____

Individuals responsible for scope and accuracy of content

Name   *Title*   *Phone*

_____

_____

_____

_____

_____

_____

_____

Existing information on program topic _____

_____

_____

_____

Script approval process_____

_____

_____

_____

Final program approval _____

_____

_____

_____

Key contact list

Event name _____

Date_____

Location _____

Time _____

Speaker(s) _____

_____

Speaker's business telephone number(s)   _____

                                                _____

                                                _____

Speaker's home telephone number(s)   _____

                                                _____

                                                _____

Speaker's local accommodations_____

_____

Caterer _____

_____

Rental company _____

_____

Florist _____

Music_____

Transportation_____

Audiovisual/lighting _____

Staff/assignments _____

_____

Other_____

_____

Responsibilities and assignments sheet

Event name_____

Event date_____

Location _____

Time_____

Letters of invitation

Staff _____

Status _____ Date_____

Note _____

Invitation list

Staff _____

Status _____ Date_____

Note _____

Printing (letters, RSVP cards, envelopes, programs, menu cards):

Staff _____

Status _____ Date_____

Note _____

Response tally

Staff _____

Status _____ Date_____

Note _____

Catering contact

Staff _____

Status _____ Date_____

Note _____

Equipment rental contact

Staff _____

Status _____ Date_____

Note _____

Venue details

Audiovisual equipment (slides, videotape, film, overhead transparencies, TV monitors, microphones, screens)

Staff _____

Status _____ Date_____

Note _____

Guest tours
Staff _____
Status _____ Date_____
Note _____
Inspections, permits
Staff _____
Status _____ Date_____
Note _____
Insurance
Staff _____
Status _____ Date_____
Note _____

Guest details
Gifts
Staff _____
Status _____ Date_____
Note _____
Meeting materials (newspapers, notepads, pens, pencils, hand-outs)
Staff _____
Status _____ Date_____
Note _____

Program
Welcoming remarks
Staff _____
Status _____ Date_____
Note _____
Luncheon/dinner remarks
Staff _____
Status _____ Date_____
Note _____
Special remarks
Staff _____
Status _____ Date_____
Note _____

Speaker coordination
Speaker(s) _____
Telephone number(s)_____
Facsimile number _____
Staff_____
Status _____ Date _____
Note _____
Seating
Staff_____
Status _____ Date _____
Note _____
Program/menu card text
Staff_____
Status _____ Date _____
Note _____
Transportation
Staff_____
Status _____ Date _____
Note _____
Music
Staff_____
Status _____ Date _____
Note _____

Parking
Valet
Self-parking accommodation
Staff_____
Status _____ Date _____
Note _____
Staff coordination
Coordinator_____
Status _____ Date _____
Note _____

Media inquiry log

Date	Caller	From	Question	Action
——	——	——	————	————
——	——	——	————	————
——	——	——	————	————
——	——	——	————	————
——	——	——	————	————
——	——	——	————	————
——	——	——	————	————
——	——	——	————	————
——	——	——	————	————
——	——	——	————	————
——	——	——	————	————
——	——	——	————	————
——	——	——	————	————
——	——	——	————	————
——	——	——	————	————
——	——	——	————	————
——	——	——	————	————
——	——	——	————	————
——	——	——	————	————
——	——	——	————	————
——	——	——	————	————
——	——	——	————	————
——	——	——	————	————
——	——	——	————	————
——	——	——	————	————
——	——	——	————	————
——	——	——	————	————
——	——	——	————	————
——	——	——	————	————
——	——	——	————	————
——	——	——	————	————
——	——	——	————	————
——	——	——	————	————
——	——	——	————	————
——	——	——	————	————
——	——	——	————	————
——	——	——	————	————
——	——	——	————	————

Corporate Communications Glossary

A

audiotex Voice-response application that allows users to enter and retrieve information via telephone. In response to a voice menu ("Press 1 for information about local weather. Press 2 for information about horoscopes.") Users press keys to obtain specific information.

B

beta A videotape format commonly used by professional videographers.

binding Joining groups of sheets of paper (or signatures) into a single unit or book. Common types of binding include perfect binding (utilizing adhesives), saddle-stitching (stapling), sewing, and mechanical post binding.

bleed Type, illustration or photo that prints off the edge of a trimmed page.

blind emboss A printing technique in which a bas-relief design is stamped without ink.

blueline A photographic print with type, photos, and illustrations in blue, used as a final proof in the printing process. It is prepared to show the client how the finished printed piece will look.

C

CD-ROM (compact disc—read only memory) A compact disc format created to hold text, graphics, and stereo sound. Even though they are similar to music CDs, information discs use different track formats for data. Audio and data reside on separate tracks and cannot be heard and viewed simultaneously. CD-ROMs are expected to become the basis for multimedia computers that will incorporate voice, data, and video into one desktop system.

camera-ready Artwork delivered to a printer that requires no further attention before going to the printer's camera department.

chromalins The result of a color proof process for four-color photographs. Color separation film negatives are exposed to plastic sheets so that process color [magenta (red), cyan (blue), yellow, and black] will adhere to dots on the plastic sheets. Four sheets are exposed (one for each color), treated with the separate colors, placed in register, and then laminated. These proofs are used for presentations and for checking register, printing blemishes, and size.

color key An overlay proof made up of individual acetate sheets for each color in the four-color printing process.

comps, comprehensives Visual representations of a layout, illustration, or design usually created for the client. The comp serves as a blueprint for an individual printed piece. Tight comps and loose comps refer to the degree of detail the comprehensive contains. Tight comps may approximate the finished product. Loose comps may be as simple as a pencil sketch.

copyright A property right in an original work of authorship, fixed in tangible form, which prohibits others from reproducing, adapting, distributing, performing, or displaying the protected work. To be valid, a copyrighted work must have originality and some modicum of creativity.

corporate communications Informational media produced as an integral part of daily business operations.

corporate culture The set of rules and attitudes that bind and define a business organization.

corporate image The uniform manifestations of an organization's public identity. Image includes specific logos, designs, packaging, or other recognizable company characteristics.

D

data base A collection of data structured and organized so that users may quickly find information of interest.

desktop publishing Utilizing a personal computer to produce high-quality printed materials or camera-ready components for commercial printing. Desktop publishing requires specific software, a high-speed personal computer, a full-page or two-page display monitor, and a laser printer.

duotone A printing method by which a halftone photograph is printed in two colors, most commonly black and another color. Because of the two inks, duotones display added richness and depth when compared with single-color halftones.

E

electronic mail (e-mail) The transmission of information through a network. E-mail systems may be integrated into mainframe, minicomputer, and personal computer local area networks (LANs). Users may send mail to an individual or broadcast it to selected audiences on the system.

embossing In printing, pressing out a design or words to create a readable surface.

engraving To etch a printing plate in order to produce a raised printed surface.

external communications Media created for audiences outside the organization.

F

facsimile (fax) The transmission of a printed page between remote locations. Fax machines scan a paper and send a coded image via telephone lines. The receiving machine prints a facsimile of the original. Fax machines contain a scanner, printer, and modem.

field tape Videotape shot on location or in a studio, which will be edited into a finished show.

foil stamping In printing, applying foil, instead of ink, to paper. Foils may be metallic, pigment, clear, or translucent.

four-color (full-color) Four colors, magenta (red), cyan (blue), yellow, and black are combined in varying amounts to recreate full-color photographs and illustrations.

G

gate-fold A four-page document (which equals eight panels) with foldouts on either side of the center spread.

generation The succeeding stage in reproduction from original art, negatives, or tape.

government relations The responsibility of monitoring legislation or lobbying on behalf of your company's or client's cause.

graphic standards The mechanical instruction used to institute and maintain a corporate image program.

guide track In the off-line edited version of a video, an audio track applied to accommodate a voice presentation. The script is read concurrently with the assembled video images to check pacing and sequence of the show.

H

halftone A photograph with gradations of tone formed by varying-sized dots. The more dots per inch, the crisper the photograph will appear when printed.

hickies Flaws in lithographic press work often manifested as spots or hairlike squiggles. Usually caused by dirt on the press, hardened specks of ink, or virtually any other piece of foreign matter in the ink, on the plate, or on the offset blanket.

I

internal communications Media created for employees, subsidiaries, or other audiences within an organization.

investor relations The responsibility of supplying information about your company or client to the financial community and monitoring financial markets.

L

letterpress A printing method by which metal type or plates carrying the image or printing areas are raised above the nonprinting areas. Ink rollers touch only the top surface of the raised areas. The nonprinting areas are lower and receive no ink. The inked image is transferred directly to the paper.

logo A graphic mark or symbol created to represent an individual, company, product, or service.

M

master tape The finished videotape from which copies are made.

media relations The responsibility of representing your company or client in the press, acting as liaison between the media and your client or company, as well as supplying information to media outlets.

mission statement An organization's stated values, beliefs, functions, goals, and purposes.

multi-image show   slide shows enhanced with other media such as live performers or video.

O

off-line edit   The first stage of video editing. Video images from field tapes are assembled sequentially. Equivalent to a rough cut of a film.

offset lithography   The most common form of lithographic printing. The image areas and the nonimage area exist on the same printing plate separated by chemical repulsion. To print, the ink is transferred (or offset) from the plate onto a rubber blanket and then to the paper.

on-line edit   The second stage of video editing. On-line editing polishes the off-line version by adding music, special effects, narration, and other details that the shows' creators may require.

overs   In printing, a shipment of finished print work in a quantity greater than the original order specified.

P

perfect binding   Pages are glued, rather than sewn or stapled to a cover. Often used for paperback books and telephone directories.

print quality   In printing, the satisfactory relation of the ink as it is applied to the paper. Parameters include intensity of the ink, crispness of the dot structure, ink "traps" (where one color is printed over another), and aligned registration.

process color   Magenta (red), cyan (blue), yellow, and black. Combined in varying amounts, these four colors recreate full-color photographs and illustrations.

proof sheet or contact sheet   Exposed photo paper onto which film negatives have been placed in strips creating an image the exact size of the negative. Used by photographers and clients to choose the best frames for reproduction.

R

register, registration   When two or more colors precisely cover each other during the printing process.

release forms   Permission agreements signed by models or property owners authorizing the photographer to shoot and the client to print or broadcast specific images.

reproduction quality   In printing, the precision with which the proof (supplied by the printer) matches the original photograph or artwork and then matches the proof on the final printed page.

S

saddle-stitching   A binding method utilizing staples in the middle folds of printed pages. Often used for magazines, pamphlets, and booklets.

separation   A print preparation function for four-color photographs or illustrations. A separation reduces a photo or illustration into four dot patterns in anticipation of printing—one for each process color: magenta (red), cyan (blue), yellow, and black.

service mark   A word, slogan, design, picture, or any other symbol used to identify and distinguish services.

sheet-fed press A press that accepts sheets of paper as opposed to paper in a roll.

sound bite The portion of a quote used in a broadcast.

stock photos Prepared photographs available for purchase from catalogs.

T

talent Actors.

talking heads A head-and-shoulders shot on a television screen.

thermography The process of applying heated resins instead of ink to paper.

teleconference A conference of two or more people linked by telecommunications. Options are audio only, video one-way and audio the other, or audio and video both ways.

teletext Broadcasting service that transmits text to home or business television sets equipped with a teletext decoder. Not an interactive medium like videotex.

trademark A word, slogan, design, picture, or any other symbol used to identify and distinguish goods.

transparency Color slide. Also full-color translucent photographic film positive. Often a printer's preferred medium from which to make color separations for color photo printing.

two-color Usually black and a second color.

U

unders In printing, a shipment of finished print work in a quantity less than the original order specified.

V

VCR (video cassette recorder) Videotape recording and playback machine. It may accommodate several tape formats: 1-inch tape is used for mastering video recordings; 3/4-inch tape is often used for commercial and professional purposes; VHS 1/2-inch tape, initially developed for home use, is now commonly found in editing studios.

VHS (video home system) Half-inch videotape. The most common video viewing format.

velox A tradename for a printing paper made by Kodak. Often erroneously applied to other similar developing papers. A velox (with lower-case *v*) is a black-and-white print of a halftone photo image, a screened image used for photo reproduction in publications.

video news release A news release delivered to broadcast or cablecast outlets on video cassette or by satellite transmission.

videotape, format Betacam, VHS, 3/4-inch, 1-inch.

videotex Two-way, interactive television providing data transmission or information retrieval to homes or commercial venues. Among its services, videotex allows users to scan consumer service data bases, pay bills, shop from catalogs, purchase tickets, or perform banking tasks. Videotex systems carry simple graphics with limited animation.

voice mail A device to record and retrieve voice messages. There are two types of voice mail devices, stand-alone systems and integrated systems. With stand-alone systems, users can instruct the machine to forward messages, allocate voice mailboxes for specific callers, or store messages for future listening. Integrated systems will tell users if they have messages and transfer callers automatically to the user's voice mailbox. The range of voice mail options varies among manufacturers.

W

web-fed printing A roll of paper that is fed into an offset press and printed on both sides before being dried, cut, folded, and bound.

window dub A videotape that contains time codes (hours, minutes, seconds, and frames) which appear in a "window" on screen. Time codes allow video editors to find scenes numerically.

wire service A business that electronically transmits and sends information to subscribers.

work-for-hire An agreement in which the commissioning party is considered to be both the "author" and the owner of the copyright from the moment of creation of the work (illustrations, photographs, etc.).

work-in-turn An economical printing technique by which the plates for both sides of the sheet are set up side by side and run for half the desired number on a double-sized sheet of paper. The plates are left in position, but the printed sheet is turned over and run through the press again, printing the reverse side.

Index